BREATHE

NICOLE BRADDOCK BROMLEY

BREATHE

FINDING FREEDOM TO THRIVE
IN RELATIONSHIPS
AFTER CHILDHOOD SEXUAL ABUSE

MOODY PUBLISHERS
CHICAGO

All Scripture quotations, unless otherwise indicated, are taken from the *Holy Bible, New Living Translation,* copyright © 1996, 2004. Used by permission of Tyndale House Publishers, Inc., Wheaton, Illinois 60189, U.S.A. All rights reserved.

Scripture quotations marked NIV are taken from the *Holy Bible, New International Version®.* NIV®. Copyright © 1973, 1978, 1984 by International Bible Society. Used by permission of Zondervan. All rights reserved.

Scripture quotations marked NASB are taken from the *New American Standard Bible®,* Copyright © 1960, 1962, 1963, 1968, 1971, 1972, 1973, 1975, 1977, 1995 by The Lockman Foundation. Used by permission. (www.Lockman.org)

Scripture quotations marked *The Message* are from *The Message,* copyright © by Eugene H. Peterson 1993, 1994, 1995. Used by permission of NavPress Publishing Group.

Editor: Judith St. Pierre
Interior Design: Ragont Design
Cover Design: DesignWorks Group
Cover Image: iStock

Library of Congress Cataloging-in-Publication Data

Bromley, Nicole Braddock.
   Breathe : finding freedom to thrive in relationships after childhood sexual abuse / Nicole Braddock Bromley.
      p. cm.
   ISBN 978-0-8024-4865-1
   1. Child sexual abuse—Religious aspects—Christianity. 2. Women—Psychology. 3. Child sexual abuse—Psychological aspects. 4. Adult child sexual abuse victims—Rehabilitation. I. Title.

HV6570.B756 2009
248.8'6—dc22

                                                                    2009000154

We hope you enjoy this book from Moody Publishers. Our goal is to provide high-quality, thought-provoking books and products that connect truth to your real needs and challenges. For more information on other books and products written and produced from a biblical perspective, go to www.moodypublishers.com or write to:

Moody Publishers
820 N. LaSalle Boulevard
Chicago, IL 60610

1 3 5 7 9 10 8 6 4 2

Printed in the United States of America

For the heroes,
who in their desire to be Jesus with skin on,
choose to walk alongside the sexually broken
on their healing journey

CONTENTS

Much Love and Thanks . . .

To my circle of inspiration, for laughing, crying, and celebrating with me through trial and triumph. You have each left a lasting footprint on my healing journey, my ministry, and my heart.

To my faithful husband, Matthew, for your genuine heart, trustworthy character, support, and steadfast love.

To Mom, for your constant guidance, prayer, encouragement, and unconditional love.

To Jenna-Leigh Wilson, for growing with me, stretching me, and allowing me the honor of walking this journey of life with you. I am grateful for you, for your special friendship, and for the countless ways in which you have contributed to this book.

To Sara Carlisle, for your challenging conversations, wealth of wisdom, and sweet friendship.

To Vineyard Church of Columbus, for being a church that breathes. And to our small group, a place where Matt and I can get real, grow, love, and serve alongside our dear friends of faith.

To Sara Burke, for helping lighten my load as I was writing and speaking.

To Dr. Judith St. Pierre, for sharing your amazing gift of writing and editing. Once again you have helped me take all that is in my heart and crafted it into something beautiful and life-changing.

To Jennifer Lyell, Lori Raschke, and the entire Moody Publishers team, for your friendship and passionate commitment to my ministry. It has been an honor to work with such a reputable organization and all of the wonderful people who have made it that way.

To the Breath of Life, my Lord and Savior, Lover and Friend, Jesus, for breathing on me. I passionately desire to be Your hands and feet in this dark and broken world. I pray that the words found in this book will breathe Your life, Your healing, Your freedom, and Your love into those who read it.

A Place to Breathe

For as long as I can remember, I've been afraid of the dark. It's getting better, but when I'm in the dark, it still doesn't take much to make my heart pound. Even the smallest sound can make me forget to breathe. The worst moments of my childhood occurred in the dark.

In the woods.

In the attic.

In the garage.

In my bed.

I sometimes pretended that my bed was a pink, frilly boat, floating in the middle of a lake and surrounded by alligators. That last part might sound scary to you, but it wasn't to me. The alligators meant that no one could get to me.

But somehow he still did.

My stepfather did things to me that no child should ever experience. While he did them, I would hold my breath. I would force my mind to take me somewhere else and make me something else. It was as if I became part of the light fixture overhead or the ballerina on the poster by the closet door or the glass angel hanging from my window frame. I watched everything from a distance. When it was over, he would leave, telling me that I was special and that it was our little secret. Gasping for air, I would return to my bed and become me again, an abused little girl who desperately wished that the alligators were real.

Childhood sexual abuse shatters many areas of a victim's life, but perhaps the greatest damage is done in the area of our relationships. Whether the abuse was a one-time exploitation or long-term trauma, its effects impact all our adult relationships. For many of us, the physical aspects of abuse don't even compare to the relational damage we carry into adulthood.

Open, honest communication is the basis of all healthy relationships. Yet survivors of childhood sexual abuse find it very difficult to talk about what they've been through. They often tell me that they remember nights when they held their breath in fear that an abuser might be near and hear them if they spoke. What they want more than anything is to be free to breathe deeply—to fill their empty places inside with life-giving air—but they never feel safe enough to do that, so they keep silent.

In *Hush,* I described the four major steps of moving from silence to healing after childhood sexual abuse. We begin the healing journey by sharing our secret. Second, we realize that the abuse wasn't our fault, which releases us from unwarranted feelings of guilt and shame. Third, we come to understand what forgiveness really means and the difference that it can make in our life. Finally, we commit ourselves to using our story to help comfort others around us who are hurting.

Since the release of *Hush,* many of you have courageously responded to my call to break the silence surrounding childhood sexual abuse. You have committed yourselves to picking up your feet day after day as you walk toward the light at the end of the long, dark tunnel of healing. You have made huge strides on your journey, and I am so proud of all of you.

Now we move beyond *Hush,* for the simple fact is that healing is a lifelong journey. Even after we've taken these four steps, there's more healing to do. We'll never make it to the light at the end of the tunnel if we're still so afraid of the dark that we forget to breathe. Along the way, we must let stale air out and fresh air in. When we do, we enter a new stage of healing that enables us to thrive in all our relationships.

I have a passion for relationships because I've witnessed the devastating effects of bad ones and the amazing transforming power of good ones. I long to see relationships grow healthier because I know the difference they can make in the life of a survivor of childhood sexual abuse. Healthy relationships are what get us to a deeper level of healing.

Breathe is a book for survivors who are ready to work on their relationships. But it is also for those who are committed to walking alongside them on their healing journey. Compassionate people like these make up what I call a survivor's *circle of inspiration.*

Because they care, they inspire us—they literally breathe new life into us by allowing us to exhale the old and inhale the new. Together, they make up our breathing space, a safe place where we can become all that God intended us to be.

As a teenager, I wrestled with why God had allowed me to suffer the pain of childhood sexual abuse. In search of answers, I turned to the Bible to see if God had anything to say about my suffering and how I could find healing for my pain. As I read stories in Scripture about suffering people, I found myself saying, "Hey! That's me!" I could relate. I've included some of these stories in *Breathe* so that all of you who suffer, for whatever reason, can know that you are not alone and that God cares about your pain and wants to help you through it.

In addition to stories from the Bible, I've told the stories of some of the survivors I've met either in person or through e-mail. At the end of each chapter, I've also included "life letters" written by survivors or by those who have helped them heal by being part of their circle of inspiration. These stories and letters not only help explain why survivors of childhood sexual abuse act as they do, but also show the great impact a circle of inspiration can have on their healing.

My own experience has been that sexual abuse has had the greatest impact on six kinds of relationships: the ones I have had with parents, mentors, fellow followers of Jesus, friends, a spouse, and God. In turn, these relationships have had the greatest influence on me on my healing journey.

Unlike me, some of you may have adult children you can include in your circle. Others of you may not have parents, but you may have people in your life who are like parents to you, so you might put them in the category of parents. Maybe you've never dated and don't plan to marry. If that's God's will for you—great! It just means that your circle will look different than mine. Because all of us are different, our healing journeys will also be different. And because we grow and change over time, so will our circles of inspiration.

As survivors of sexual abuse, we desperately need such a circle.

It's our habitat for healing, a place of mutual speaking and listening, of learning and teaching, of supporting and being supported, of giving and receiving unconditional love. It's a place where we can finally be free to breathe.

Part One
EXHALING

A circle of inspiration is a safe space where we can quit holding our breath, a place where we can exhale the false identity, isolation, and addictions that prevent us from walking the healing path.

I want every single one of you who has experienced the pain of sexual abuse to have your own circle of inspiration. On my own healing journey, I always pictured myself walking on a path through a long, dark tunnel to the light at the end. Now I imagine each of you doing the same thing on your own healing journey. I see you gradually picking up speed and eventually running down the tunnel of healing, with your supporters lining both sides of the path and cheering you on to victory. This is a compelling image in my mind, for I know the impact each one in my own circle has had on my healing and will continue to have as I keep moving forward on my lifelong journey toward wholeness.

When you find that it is no longer an option to walk this road alone—yes, you eventually will—I hope you'll decide to create and cultivate your circle of inspiration. Creating a network of caring people who are willing to be there and to listen and love and support you plays a crucial role as you tread the pathway to life.

1 GETTING Real

Getting Real Getting Real Getting Real Getting Real Real...Real

THE RIGHTEOUS HATE WHAT IS FALSE.

—Proverbs 13:5 NIV

As a child, I loved to drag a large cardboard box from the garage into the house, climb in, and then cover the opening with a big blanket. The blanket was my protection. It meant that no one could get in and that I was safe. I would surround myself with stuffed animals and dolls to keep me company. We would read books, listen to music, or just hang out together. However, I couldn't hide in that box for long because the blanket cut off my supply of fresh air. I had to pull back the blanket now and then so I could breathe.

SOMEONE WHO NEEDED
to Find the Right Road

Matthew 9:20–22, Mark 5:25–29, and Luke 8:43–48 all tell the story of a woman who had been bleeding for twelve years. She had spent every cent she had on doctors, but they hadn't been able to heal her. In fact, she had just gotten worse. The constant bleeding meant debilitating weakness. Worse, it meant that she was ritually unclean, an untouchable social outcast. She couldn't maintain normal, healthy relationships, and so she suffered in isolation. She had no one to care about her or support her with compassionate understanding.

One day this suffering woman heard that Jesus was passing through her town. Everyone knew about the miracles He had been doing, and soon a great crowd gathered and followed Him. Most people wouldn't have known about the woman's condition unless she told them, so she was able to act as if everything was normal and mingle with the crowd.

Hiding among the swarm of people, the woman worked her

way closer and closer to Jesus, convinced that if she could just get close enough to touch His garment, she would be healed. Finally, she came up behind Him, reached out her hand, and touched the hem of His robe. Then, just as quickly, she melted back into the crowd. For twelve years, she had been faking it. And even though she now knew that her bleeding had stopped, she was afraid of what would happen if everyone knew that she had been unclean. She felt ashamed, embarrassed, and afraid. And so she hid and *held her breath.*

Jesus, however, wouldn't allow her to continue to hide. Knowing that power had gone out of Him, He immediately turned around and began looking for the woman so He could invite her to come out and *breathe.*

CAN YOU RELATE?

Before I began my healing journey, I was like that woman, holding my breath and hiding who I really was. Instead of speaking up, I tried to be someone else. I strove to be a superathlete with perfect grades and a big flashy smile. That was my cover, like the blanket over my box when I was a child. But even when I was in a crowd, I found myself alone and afraid. My mask made me feel a little safer, but as long as I wore it, I breathed the same stale notion that I would always be what my stepfather had made me.

I was relying on my false identity to change me from the outside in. I longed to become what others saw on the outside and liked. But becoming authentic can never happen that way. It has to happen from within. I needed to take off the blanket—and not just for a quick breather. I had to take it off for good. Finally I decided that I was going to find me. Little by little, I was going to get real. I was going to breathe.

When I began working on getting real, I can remember asking myself what I was looking for. At first, the only thing I knew for sure was what I *wasn't* looking for—anything fake. I hate fake. I never again wanted to be someone I wasn't. I wanted to be free to be who I really was when nobody was watching. However, I wasn't sure how being me would affect others. I was afraid that if they saw the real me, they'd no longer like me. Yes, I wanted to be real, but the risk seemed too great.

Millions of people like the bleeding woman and me are alive today—and fighting to stay alive. Inside there's a constant battle raging between our greatest desire and our greatest fear. We want so much to just be real and lay ourselves out there, but we're ashamed and afraid of what others will think, so we shrink back. The pressure is always there to keep quiet and pretend that things are fine, all the while hoping that somehow, someone will see the real person deep inside and invite her to come out and breathe.

WHY WE HIDE
What's Inside

Every time my stepfather touched me, I felt as if I was losing a small piece of me. As I got smaller and smaller, our secret seemed to grow bigger and bigger. The silence was cramming all the small, shattered pieces of me into some secret, shameful box that I hoped no one would ever open.

I am not alone. Every day I meet or receive e-mails from people who have been sexually abused and have kept silent about it. When Ryan was six years old, a teenage neighbor boy molested him. Ryan kept this secret for years. Now he says, "One of the reasons I hid the abuse was because I was ashamed of my inner self, the part that no other person sees or knows except for God." Jackie never talked about the abuse she suffered at the hands of her teacher because she felt ashamed and alone and didn't think that talking about it would change that. Many survivors who have lived in silence falsely believe that talking about their abuse will not only do nothing to reduce their shame and isolation, but that it will actually make things worse.

Survivors of childhood sexual abuse long to be accepted for who we are. As children, we never felt accepted because we believed something was wrong with us. We thought that something about us was bad and deserved punishment. Now as adults, it doesn't make sense to us that someone would accept us just because we're not being abused anymore. So we decide to become someone else—someone others will accept, maybe even love. We figure that people will like a fake version of us, as long as it's what they want to see.

But even though our façade helps win us the acceptance of others, we feel exactly the same inside. Contrary to what we believed, we do not feel better. We still can't accept ourselves, for we don't even know the real us. We long to know who we really are. It's an obsessive thought for us. A fantasy. But we find that we fear it just as much as we long for it. It seems easier to just keep faking it.

When I decided to get real, I took small, quick breaths of fresh air. A little trust here. A little openness there. I kept the blanket off just long enough to know that I was making progress. But as I kept on working at getting real, I began to realize that what I was looking for was a community where I could heal, where I could find acceptance, love, purpose, and hope. I was looking for a circle of inspiration.

When Jesus began His public ministry, He chose twelve men to accompany Him on His journey as He fulfilled God's purpose for His life. For three years, twelve of His disciples were closer to Him than His own family was, even though He knew that one day one of them would betray Him. When that day came, Jesus didn't hide His pain. He didn't fake it and pretend that everything was all right. In the garden of Gethsemane, He gave three members of His inner circle the opportunity to support and comfort Him in His suffering. Although His disciples failed Him that night, the fact that even Jesus needed the support of others shows us how important it is to have a circle of inspiration.

Creating your own circle can take a while. Most of the time, no one will know that you even need this kind of support until you speak up about it. Hence my passion and focus on empowering survivors to break the silence. It also takes time to build relationships by learning to trust again and allowing others to know you.

Your circle may seem small or even nonexistent at this point. You may still be holding your breath, too afraid to breathe. But that can change. Just remember that, like Jesus, you get to choose the people you want to be in your circle. You're the only one who decides who will get to hear your story. Only you can determine who will have the high honor of getting to know the real you.

ONLY YOU can determine who will have the high honor of getting to know the real you.

I remember that in my teenage years—before the entire world knew that I had been sexually abused— I was very strategic about telling people my story. I thought it over very carefully before I told someone. I wouldn't tell just anyone. The person I allowed to know this part of me had to be someone very special, someone I could really trust.

We need to find people we trust—or people we can begin to try to trust—and share our story with them. This is where our healing journey begins and where our circle of inspiration starts to grow. So to begin to form your circle, start with someone you feel you can trust. Chances are, this person will be caring and compassionate, someone who is willing to reach out to you in your pain. That's why you feel you can trust them. Then find the courage to tell them a little bit of your story.

GETTING REAL ABOUT
Sexual Abuse

Recently I received an e-mail that touched my heart. "When I listened to you speak," Dawn wrote, "I felt the same way inside as I do when I watch a movie and something happens on the screen that seems so real. I realize that I've been holding my breath, and I finally begin to breathe again. It's a moment when it feels as if the truth is supposed to be out there in the open for everyone to see. Embarrassment or fear isn't able to creep into my mind because I'm not thinking about the people around me. I'm focused only on what's in front of me and what's inside of me."

Like Dawn, many of the people who listen to me speak say that they identify with me because they can tell that I understand their situation, whatever it may be. They can tell that I care about what they went through. Compassionate understanding is something I strive for in my everyday walk with others and something I want all survivors to experience. I long to see them in safe relationships where they are finally able to accept that healing and freedom is found in being real.

Even though I'm now at a point where I feel great about life and don't have to struggle every day with the pain of my past, I'm always conscious of my need for authenticity. To be authentic, I have to remember the abuse I suffered and allow myself to feel the heaviness of the pain. This doesn't mean dwelling on the past or reliving it for no reason. And it certainly doesn't mean wallowing in self-pity. The purpose of remembering is to show other survivors that I understand them and that they can trust me to relate to their pain. This means that I also have to talk about the awful reality of childhood sexual abuse.

By the age of eighteen, one in three girls and one in six boys will be victims of childhood sexual abuse. We are living amidst the rubble and shards of a sexually broken world, yet most people still deny the reality of the numbers of abused living among us. Unlike the survivors of natural or man-made disasters, survivors of sexual abuse seldom have heroes rushing in to rescue them. In fact, those who should be their protectors are often their abusers. And those around them either do nothing or tell them to *hush*. If they speak at all, it's to condemn the victim, not the perpetrator.

Sexually abused children seldom have the sympathetic ear of even one person, much less a group. They have no supporters to rally around them to help protect and preserve their bodies, minds, and souls. But, as this secret—the best-kept secret in our country— begins to be exposed, more and more concerned and caring people are reaching out and making a difference in the lives of survivors.

The tragedy of sexual abuse draws together survivors and the people who truly care about them. It unites those ready to begin healing from their pain and those who are willing to be part of their circle of inspiration. That circle begins with just two people: a survivor who is willing to get real about his experiences and someone who cares enough to want to help him heal.

NEVER TURNING our heads or hearts from those who have been victimized marks the beginning of cultural change.

The sad but honest truth is that even when we do care, we so often come up with all kinds of reasons why we can't reach out.

"It's too big of a problem; I can't put a dent in it."

"I don't know how to even begin."

"What will people think of me if they see me hanging out with her?"

"It's too time consuming."

"My nails are drying."

"The playoffs are on TV."

But let's get real. If we do nothing, this evil will survive. In reaching out, you're not only fulfilling a great need in someone else's life, you're also sparking a movement. I have found that for each person I encourage, another encourager is born. As more and more people walk with a survivor on the road of healing, that survivor in turn will reach out to others.

Never turning our heads or hearts from those who have been victimized marks the beginning of cultural change. Together, we can make a huge difference by refusing to keep the secret that is shattering relationships. To me this is a revolution: survivors removing the cover, stepping out of the box, and getting real by relating to people who are willing to come alongside them in their pain and be part of their healing process.

THE REST of the Story

Although everyone around Jesus denied touching Him, He kept looking for the woman. Finally, she came forward. Trembling with fear, she fell down before Him, took a deep breath, and spoke up.

When the woman found enough courage to stop hiding just for the moment it took to reach out for healing, God changed a situation that had been a problem for years. Sometimes when we've tried everything we know to heal our own pain but fail, we're tempted to give up. But if we have faith in Him and ask Him to help us, He has the power to heal us.

The bleeding woman knew that this was true, and when she acknowledged the truth about herself, Jesus also told her the truth—she was His daughter and she didn't need to hide or pretend any more. "'Daughter,' [Jesus] said to her, 'your faith has made you well. Go in peace'" (Luke 8:48). The woman got healed by her faith, but she got real by getting into a relationship with the One who could help her.

It's easy for survivors to believe that they are terrible, rotten, unclean people. But that's not the way Jesus sees it. To Him, there's no such thing as an unclean person; there's just someone who needs His healing touch. Whoever He touches becomes clean. When Jesus called the woman "daughter," He showed that He is willing to be in relationship with the least, the last, and the lost—the very people that society often considers unclean. He is not only willing to be in relationship with them; He loves them as His own.

We only find out who we really are in relationship to others. This means that if we want to find our real selves, we have to stop holding our breath so we can tell others the truth about us and what we've been through. Are you tired of hiding? Of faking your way through life? If so, it's time to get real. It's time to find and embrace your true identity—the true you, the person God made you to be. Jesus is inviting you to remove the blanket, step out of the box—and breathe!

A Life Letter

Dear Fellow Survivor . . .

I am a victim of childhood sexual abuse.

Sometime in my late thirties, I began to acknowledge that some of the memories of childhood lingering in the recesses of my mind were connected with sexual abuse. Once I recognized it for what it was, all the pieces of the puzzle of my life began to fit together, and it was easy to see how it had affected who I had become. I realized that the aftereffects of these traumas had led to major life decisions that left me broken, wounded, and empty inside. At the same time, I looked around and discovered that God had already placed in my life people who could, and would, help me heal. They became my circle of inspiration.

A group of women forming a prayer group invited me to join them. As we prayed together and got real with one another, my prayer partners acted as a sounding board, held me accountable, and prayed with me for answers. Eventually I felt safe enough to share some of my experiences with my husband. By providing me with healthy nurturing, protection, and support, he is playing a very important role as I work through my most painful memories, which I am just now remembering. In this stage of healing, I have also added a therapist to my circle to provide crucial, professional guidance.

Repressed memories have come forward within the safety net of my circle. I tell you this not to frighten you, but to show you how much deeper the healing can go when you have others supporting you and encouraging you. Ironically, moving forward in life entails looking back. It means processing what's taken place in the past in order to improve the outcome of the future. Any good business analyst does this to grow a company. He pulls together a group of experts to discuss how every detail of their operation affects the outcome. This is even more crucial for growing a person, especially for overcoming the deeply rooted pain of sexual sin. I see my circle of inspiration as my "analysts." I confer with them and discuss the details of my past with them as we work together toward a new improved me.

This new person isn't some stereotypical image of what I should be like. This person is the one God knit together in my mother's womb, the one whose days are written in His book of life (Psalm 139). This person is the one He created me to be, in all the fullness and freedom He intended, unpolluted by the sin committed against me. Now, more than ten years into my healing journey, I am closer and closer to being the real me—all because I refused to allow the life-altering experience of childhood sexual abuse to dictate my future in the way that it had shaped my past.

Look around. Who do you love and trust? Who has God already placed in your life as your circle of influence? Nurture those relationships. Spend time with those people. Be real with them. Share with them where you've been. Allow them to be a part of where you want to go. And may the Lord bless your journey.

—Cynthia

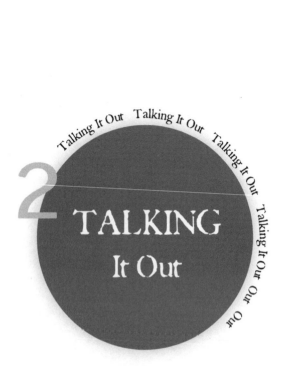

2

TALKING
It Out

HOW GOOD IS A TIMELY WORD.

—Proverbs 15:23 NIV

When life gets difficult, survivors often stop communicating. Just when we most need to connect with the people who can support us, we withdraw, clam up, and try to go it alone. Yet in isolating ourselves, we take a step backward on the path to healing, for the members of our circle of inspiration are the very breaths of life that can help us survive the difficult times.

God wants us to lean on each other as we seek His healing. We can't do this alone. We need each other. We need community. We need safe relationships in which we can talk about our day-to-day struggles. Yes, it's frightening to think of laying out all of our "junk," all of our burdens, for others to see, but we'll never find true freedom or healing if we keep it all inside and try to deal with it alone. In fact, if we don't talk about it, it will only grow bigger and more life threatening, like an unseen, untreated tumor in our lungs that slowly cuts off our air supply.

SOMEONE WHO NEEDED
to Talk It Out

Hannah was depressed. It happened this time every year. She was traveling with her husband, Elkanah, and his other wife, Peninnah, from their home in Ephraim to worship and sacrifice to God at the tabernacle at Shiloh. Along the way, Peninnah made fun of Hannah because she was barren. While Peninnah had many children, Hannah had none. She already felt like a failure, and Peninnah made her feel worse. Powerless to change her situation, she succumbed to feelings of worthlessness and depression. Reduced to tears, she wouldn't even eat.

Her husband gently reproved her for her grief. "Why are you crying, Hannah?" Elkanah would ask. "Why aren't you eating? Why be downhearted just because you have no children? You have me— isn't that better than having ten sons?" (1 Samuel 1:8). Elkanah thought that it was time for Hannah to get over it and move on. Although he loved her, he didn't really understand what was going on with her. Neither did Eli, the priest.

One day at Shiloh when Hannah went to pray, Eli was sitting at his usual place beside the entrance of the tabernacle. Hannah was in deep distress, and she cried inconsolably as she prayed. Eli was watching her, and when he saw her lips move but didn't hear a sound, he assumed she had been drinking.

"'Must you come here drunk?' he demanded. 'Throw away your wine!'" (v.14).

Until now, Hannah has been suffering in silence. There's no indication that she responded to Peninnah's taunts or that she tried to help Elkanah understand her pain. She had spoken only to God in prayer, but now she spoke to another person.

"'Oh no, sir!' she replied. 'I haven't been drinking wine or anything stronger. But I am very discouraged, and I was pouring out my heart to the Lord. Don't think I am a wicked woman! For I have been praying out of great anguish and sorrow.'"

"'In that case,' Eli said, 'go in peace! May the God of Israel grant the request you have asked of him.'"

"'Oh, thank you, sir!' she exclaimed. Then she went back and began to eat again, and she was no longer sad'" (vv.15–18).

CAN YOU RELATE?

Krystyna never told her mother, Janice, about the night her own brother raped her. She isolated herself from her family and kept this secret for years. In her heart, Krystyna blamed her mom for not protecting her, even though Janice wasn't even aware of what had happened.

For her part, Janice felt neglected and unloved because from the time her daughter was a teenager, she never showed her any affection. Krystyna's secret was hurting not only her, but also Janice, who wanted a loving relationship with her daughter but felt that Krystyna did not. Not knowing what else to do, Janice finally wrote her daughter a letter in which she expressed her feelings. She asked if she had done anything that made Krystyna love her less and if there was anything she could do to help her love her more.

When she read her mother's letter, Krystyna found the courage to open up and express the anger and feelings of betrayal that had led her to push her mom away many years earlier. Only through this intimate sharing were they both able to understand the root of Krystyna's behavior and begin to walk together on the road of healing and restoration. Communication was the key.

You know what happens when we make assumptions, right? It makes fools of us all. When Eli made a false assumption about Hannah, he responded to her tearful prayer by condemning her instead of ministering to her. If Hannah hadn't spoken up, he would never have known what the real problem was and how he could help her. I see this all the time in relationships. Our human nature leads us to respond as Eli did. We're much quicker to conclude that people who seem different or in distress are messed-up losers than we are to reach out in love to find out what the real issue is with them.

Instead of assuming anything about people, we need to communicate with them. To truly be in relationship with others, we must truly know them, and that kind of knowledge comes only through communication. Not just the superficial "How are you?" "Good. How about you?" kind of stuff. We have to communicate in a way that reveals our heart and allows others to reveal theirs. Yet, for survivors such communication can be extremely difficult.

WHY WE CLAM UP

Communication is crucial in relationships. Having gotten married not too long ago, I know this to be oh, so true! Yet dialoguing with a survivor can often be difficult because we fear how others will react to what we say. Will they look at us differently, feel obligated to show us sympathy, or tell us to *hush*? Will they refuse to believe us? Condemn us? Pity us? These are the reactions that survivors fear the most. And though we often know that telling our secret has the power to heal, our fears keep us quiet and prevent the very healing we desire.

For many of us, a relationship can seem like a dangerous place to be. Even though we may have strong feelings of affection or friendship, we're afraid of what letting down our guard will do, so we prefer to run. We distance ourselves in order to protect ourselves from being hurt again. This puts others on the defensive as well, and our relationships become tense and controlled. This can confuse those who care for us and leave them feeling hurt or angry, even to the point of distancing themselves in return. Add to the mix our low feelings of self-worth and mistrust of others, and you'll often find us isolating ourselves from community.

The effects of childhood abuse are manifold, but there are two in particular that can lead to isolation and prevent healing: denial and anger.

Denial is a natural defense mechanism that helps children survive abuse. Unfortunately, as abused children grow up, some of us continue to rely on it because we don't trust our own perceptions. Forced to deny what our own senses tell us is healthy and proper in relationships, we do everything we can to convince ourselves that what happened to us was normal or "not that bad."

Hilary's cousin molested her for five straight summers. Her cousin's family was very well respected, and Hilary thought that no one would believe that her cousin or anyone else in the family would do such a thing. So she pretended it away. Only now, at the age of twenty-four, is she beginning to recognize the effects that her denial has had on her life. It seems that she can't keep a friend for more than a month. Whenever anyone shows genuine interest in her, she runs and hides. The denial that helped Hilary survive her childhood now isolates her, preventing her from having healthy adult relationships.

Some survivors will defend the one who hurt them by minimizing or rationalizing what happened, or by blaming themselves for their abuser's devastating choices. Such denial can actually lead to more abusive relationships in adulthood.

Like many survivors, Jamila made excuses for the behavior of her abuser instead of placing the blame where it belonged. She often made comments to her friend Shaunti about how her dad was always drunk when he raped her. When Shaunti would tell her that nothing can excuse a father for treating his daughter that way, Jamila would say something like, "Well, I should've known better than to sleep in my bed when he was drinking. I should've gone to my neighbor's house."

Now Jamila finds herself in relationships that reinforce the lie that the abuse in her childhood was somehow her fault. She acts as though she deserves nothing better because that's how she views herself, and she attracts people who want to take advantage of her in every way.

Anger is another issue that isolates survivors. While it is certainly an appropriate response to what happened to us, the problem is that it often burns so hot within us that it finally boils over onto those nearest to us and burns up our relationships. Once all our friendships are toast, we are left all alone, struggling in isolation.

Molested by his uncle, Parker never felt that he could talk about what happened or how it affected him. He bottled up all the anger he had toward his uncle, himself, and his parents, although he desperately wanted his mom and dad to see his need and reach out to him. His anger isolated him, and he grew up thinking that he couldn't trust anyone. He vowed to never trust again, to never love again, and to never get close enough to anyone to love him in return.

Jack told me that he spent most of his first three years of college in his dorm room, cut off from social life and thus the opportunity to grow in relationships with others. He didn't care, though, because relationships were exactly what he was afraid of. As a child, Jack had put all of his trust in his father, and he had seen what that got him: pain and betrayal.

I can relate to both Parker and Jack, for I was there for a season of my life as well. It wasn't that I isolated myself outwardly. In fact I was quite the social butterfly. But inwardly I wasn't willing to let others know me too deeply or to soften my heart enough to have an emotional relationship. I was a "tough girl" who would never let myself cry or be vulnerable. I couldn't give anyone an open door to bring more pain or betrayal into my life. I thought that if I could wall off my heart from others, no one could get close enough to me to hurt me. At the time, being tough seemed to be the way to conquer my fears. But in the end, I found that it only added to my fears and prevented the life of freedom I longed for.

While it's essential to know why and how survivors isolate themselves, this knowledge isn't what brings the most healing. Healing occurs when we put what we know into practice. This means that survivors must have opportunities to relate to people who will listen and give them good, supportive feedback.

HELPING A SURVIVOR
Talk It Out

Sandra's youth pastor sexually abused her when she was an adolescent. She told her secret to her best friend, Jane, while they were in college. Jane didn't really have anything to say—she didn't respond one way or the other—so Sandra could never tell how Jane felt about it. Sandra hoped that Jane understood that her abuser was responsible, but deep in her heart she wondered if Jane was thinking that she had encouraged it or wanted it. Sandra said that any response would have better than none. "What I need is dialogue," she said, "not just blank stares."

As someone who is hearing a survivor share his secret—perhaps for the very first time—you need to understand these fears and react to them in a way that will help him feel safe. Your immediate response to his story is one of the greatest impacts you will have on his life.

Communication means two things: speaking and listening. But I would agree with James that we should be "quick to listen, slow to speak" (James 1:19). In relationships with survivors, we need to listen first and then think carefully before we speak.

While you're listening to a survivor's story, remember that nonverbal communication is very important. Things like physical proximity, eye contact, facial expressions, hand gestures, and posture speak as loudly as words. Sitting too far away from a survivor as she tells you her story can make her think that you don't want to be too close to her because you consider her gross or dirty. Not keeping eye contact can make it seem as if her story isn't that important.

If you're sitting on the same couch, sit about an arm's-length distance away, and listen intently. Keep good eye contact. Lean in as you listen to his words of pain of betrayal. Nod your head in agreement and allow the hurt you feel for him to shine through your eyes. This kind of nonverbal communication will send a clear message that what happened to him was horrible, that what his abuser did was wrong, and that he didn't deserve it.

Don't assume that a sexual abuse survivor doesn't want to be touched. Yes, it is true that this is the last thing some survivors want. If their deepest pain has come through touch, they may not be ready for you to use touch as a way to show them your love for them. The best thing to do is ask. After reassuring your friend of your love for her, tell her you would like to give her a big hug but that you want to make sure that it's okay with her. By doing this, you're giving her control over touch—something she never had as a child. She couldn't choose back then, but you can give her the choice now.

Some people—like me!—can't seem to go without touch. It's one of my main love languages. We have feeling in our skin for a reason, and part of that reason, I believe, is to feel loved through safe and warm touch. Touch can dramatically change a person's outlook on life.

Nate is one of the many sexual abuse survivors who struggle with the lie that he is dirty because of what happened to him as a child. He told me that one of the ways his circle has helped counteract that lie is through touch. He realized that if people can touch him in such a safe and loving way, it must mean that he isn't as gross as he once thought. Nate will never forget the first time a true friend gave him a hug and an encouraging word. It made him feel clean and pure again.

Staci signed up for an individual appointment with me the afternoon after I had spoken at the college she attended. At the end of our time together, I asked if I could pray for her. She said yes. I asked if I could hold her hand as I prayed. She said yes. After we prayed, she thanked me. I hugged her, and she went off to her next class.

Weeks later, Staci sent me an e-mail telling me how much it meant that I had listened to her, told her that it wasn't her fault, cried with her, and prayed for her. But she said that what meant the most to her was my willingness to hold her hand and hug her. She said when she thinks about it, she can still feel the warmth of my hands around hers. She longs for healthy touch. It is one thing that makes Staci and many others of us feel loved and accepted.

In communicating with survivors at the level they deserve, we must be in touch with our own thoughts and feelings. If our words don't match what we feel in our heart, the people we're reaching out to won't believe what we say or trust us. In that case, it isn't possible to have a healthy, healing relationship with them.

Just as you need to share how you feel, you should encourage a survivor to share what he feels. Many times survivors aren't good at telling others how they feel or what upsets them. Fearing how others may respond, they tend to crawl back into their box, and that does them no good at all. While I'm encouraging another survivor to open up about his feelings, I picture myself holding a cocoon in my hands. As I listen to the struggle going on inside and show my concern and interest in his story, little by little a breathtaking butterfly starts to emerge, beginning the process of becoming all God has called him to be.

As a result of an open dialogue with Shaunti, Jamila is just beginning to discern light from dark. She is learning to distinguish between the truth and lies and to discover her true identity. As she gains self-confidence, she will be able to make better, healthier decisions in other relationships.

In his senior year, Jack finally faced reality. He had no friends, no family, and no one else to support him. He was lonely and still hurting—maybe even more than ever. The isolation that he believed would fix his problem had only added to it. Little by little, Jack began to engage in the world again. He joined a club on campus, and now he has friends he cares about and who care about him. He's in relationship with a group of people who support one another in all the ups and downs of life.

"I've been blown away lately by how telling my story brings people closer together," Elissa wrote me. "As much as I trusted the women in my Bible study group, I was terrified to tell them my story. At the same time, there was a bee in my britches that just wouldn't leave me alone. It kept bugging me to tell secrets that had been rotting deep inside my heart for thirty-seven years. I thought that revealing these secrets would destroy me, but God had other plans. Once I told those trusted friends my story, something miraculous happened: others started telling their stories."

Being connected to a group of supportive and loving people is vital for survivors. Just spending time in such a community can break down their sense of isolation and the false belief that they are somehow "different" or "damaged." So step out and have coffee with that person God has laid on your heart. Send her an encouraging note in the mail. Listen to her story. Give her a warm hug. As more and more people walk with a survivor on the road of healing, that survivor in turn will reach out to others.

Just as one abusive relationship can completely distort an abused child's development, so just one healthy relationship can lead to a tremendous amount of healing. The more, the better, of course. But if just one person is willing to enter a tender dialogue with a broken survivor of abuse, that hurting person will be well on her way to the light at the end of the tunnel.

THE REST of the Story

Even though Hannah's situation hadn't changed at all, her conversation with Eli lifted her out of her depression. Hannah had no way of knowing that her story was going to have a happy ending. She didn't know that the Lord was going to give her not only the son she prayed for that day—the prophet Samuel, no less!—but five more children as well. All she knew was that after she talked about her inner hurt, her depression lifted. She stopped crying, and her deep sadness dissipated. She had talked out her pain, and even though Eli didn't even know what Hannah had asked God to do for her, his words of encouragement gave her hope.

Talking it out in prayer helped Hannah focus on God's power instead of her powerlessness, and talking about it with Eli allowed him to support her by adding his prayer to hers. Talking about what was going on inside of her made all the difference.

Talking it out with people who care can make a huge difference in the lives of survivors as well. Folks who are holding in a lot of secret pain walk by us every day, and it would provide them with a great deal of relief to talk about it with someone who really cared. We all have some type of baggage in our lives, and many of us are looking around, just waiting for someone who cares enough to minister to us by reaching out and providing us a safe place where we can set down our bags and talk it out. Besides giving us hope, talking it out can help keep unhealthy ways of coping from becoming death-dealing addictions.

A Life Letter

Dear Fellow Survivor . . .

My church doesn't have a youth group, so last spring when a girl in my art class invited me to go to her church, I decided to start attending hers. I soon grew very close with the girls in the group and with Jillian, the girls' youth minister.

One day while I was at the church helping Jillian paint a banner for youth camp, she asked me how I was doing. I don't know what came over me, but I told her I was really struggling with something from my past. I didn't want to talk about it then, so she let it drop. But she must have realized that it was something serious, because as the summer went on, she kept asking me how I was doing. I knew she wasn't going to stop until I told her the truth, but I didn't want to break the silence.

I loved my life, and I wasn't willing to sacrifice it all. I made good grades, I had amazing friends, I was getting ready for college, and I had just won a state soccer championship. Yet my secret was always there, reminding me of the pain and the lies. For years I had been begging God to do something, anything, to break these chains, and now He told me I had to sacrifice it all for Him and speak.

So last July I found myself in a Sunday school room with Jillian, my stomach in knots, trying to find the strength to tell her the secret I had sworn to take to my grave. Finally my sprit won the battle with my flesh, and I spoke. I told Jillian that my father had molested me from the time I was in third grade to about the beginning of sixth grade. When my mom was gone, he would ask me to sleep in his bed with him, and I knew what was coming. I ended up terrified, angry, and broken, but I never told anyone. I learned to hide it so well that at times I even hid it from myself. But the closer I got to God, the more convicted I became that I had to set the truth free.

The next day Jillian asked my mom to come to the church,

and I sat down with the two of them and told my mom the truth. She cried and got angry, then asked my father to come to the church. As I waited for my mom to come back into the room with my father, I asked God to deliver me. Jillian asked me if I was ready to face him, and I shook my head no. So she grabbed my hand and we ran down the steps to the basement, where she stashed me in a Sunday school room. Later my mom got me and sent me to my grandmother's for three days.

At first my dad denied everything, but my mom said that I was not a liar and that she believed me. When my dad denied everything to my face, I began to ask myself if I had made it all up. I have never been so angry or confused. About a week later my parents and I went a Christian counselor, and my dad confessed. "Carrie, I am so sorry," he said. "It's not your fault; it's not your fault." Then he walked out of the room crying.

When I heard the words that I had been waiting years to hear, I felt so much freedom. It was a beautiful moment. However, I learned very quickly that it was only the beginning of the healing journey. I'm still healing, still struggling, and still fighting to break down the walls that have separated me from the members of my family.

God is raising up a generation that is refusing to be silent. As a part of His plan, He is providing people like me with a circle of inspiration filled with people like Jillian. Together we are breaking the bondage created by childhood sexual abuse.

—Carrie

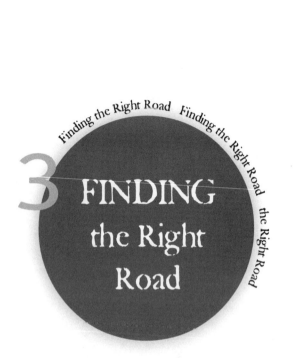

3

FINDING
the Right
Road

THERE IS A PATH BEFORE EACH PERSON
THAT SEEMS RIGHT, BUT IT ENDS IN DEATH.

—Proverbs 14:12

Times of solitude are important for all of us. Much healing can occur in alone times as God draws us nearer to Him, encourages us, and communicates His vision for our life. But as Martin Luther once said, too much solitude isn't good for us. "When we are alone, the worst and saddest things come to mind," Luther wrote. "We reflect in detail upon all sorts of evils. And if we have encountered adversity in our lives, we dwell upon it as much as possible, magnify it, think that no one is so unhappy as we are, and imagine the worse possible consequences."

Spending too much time alone can cause those of us who are hurting to focus only on our pain and then look for a way to fix it. As survivors of sexual abuse, we feel a *lot* of pain. To ease it, we often turn onto the path of addiction. Instead of choosing the path of healing by seeking support from those who can breathe fresh air into our lungs, we push them away and rely on a phony substitute for a circle of inspiration. As a way to get rid of our inner pain, an addiction can seem right at first. However, it ultimately leads to more wounds and, for some, death.

Jesus said, "Enter through the narrow gate. For wide is the gate and broad is the road that leads to destruction, and many enter through it. But small is the gate and narrow the road that leads to life, and only a few find it" (Matthew 7:13–14 NIV). I believe that only a few survivors find the road leading to life because most of them believe that the path of addiction is the only way open to them. This is a lie of the Enemy. There is a way out. There is a road that leads to life and freedom from your pain.

SOMEONE WHO NEEDED
to Find the Right Road

The New Testament tells the story of a woman who found the right road in a dramatic way. The story begins with Jesus sitting in the temple, teaching the crowd that has gathered around Him. John says that as Jesus was speaking, the Jewish religious leaders dragged in a woman and put her before Him. "'Teacher,' they said to Jesus, 'this woman was caught in the act of adultery. The law of Moses says to stone her. What do you say?'" (John 8:4–5).

John goes on to explain why the religious leaders were making a spectacle of this poor woman: they were just trying to corner Jesus (v. 6). If He said that the woman shouldn't be stoned, they could accuse Him of false teaching. If He said that she should be stoned, they could accuse Him of sedition, for the Romans didn't allow the Jews to carry out capital punishment. Jesus' enemies thought they had Him for sure, and they could hardly wait for His answer.

But Jesus didn't answer right away. Instead, He stooped down and began to write something in the dirt.

I can't help but wonder, what Jesus was writing. Perhaps it was Deuteronomy 22:22, which says that both parties to adultery were to be stoned. Or was He perhaps writing down the story of the woman who stood before Him?

Maybe as a young girl she had dreamed of finding the perfect mate, only to have her dream turn into a nightmare when a respected member of the community, someone she loved and trusted, began to sexually abuse her. What if, as she grew up, she turned to sex to try to feel better about herself?

CAN YOU RELATE?

Noelle is an admitted sex addict. "From the time I was born," she says, "the people who were supposed to love and protect me rejected me, used me, and abused me. I think I've clung so tightly to sex because when I was little, it was the way I was told I was loved. Now having sex is the only way I know to escape from the brokenness

I feel inside because of my miserable experiences."

Noelle longs for love, but she's afraid to love, so she settles for sex. She treats sex the same way the guys she dates treat it—as if it's no big thing. Letting guys touch her, grab her, and do whatever they want with her has become a kind of game, one in which she tells herself that she can't get hurt.

But the truth is that it does hurt her. It leaves her feeling empty, helpless, and used. "I haven't wanted to face those feelings," Noelle says, "so I haven't let my mind go there. To admit that I'm weak and that sex tears away at my soul has been too hard for me. I've been afraid of what would happen if I stepped out from behind the lie that promiscuous sex doesn't hurt me. It seems that the only way to not feel pain is to inflict more pain."

Emotionally starved for true affection, Noelle admits that she's given herself away too many times in the hope of finding love. "I'm tired of being held hostage by the abuse I feel I deserve," she says. "However, my fear of being alone seems greater than my disgust with myself. Sex has become like a drug that numbs the pain of my loneliness, and I'm afraid of what would happen if I let go of it. I'm afraid that without sex, I would have no social life, no fun, no comfort, no way to ease the sting of the void inside my soul. I would have no way to fulfill my desire for attention and love."

Sadly, the only path that Noelle can see is the destructive one. Alone in the dark, she can't see Jesus, much less hold on to Him, and to relieve her pain she turns to the false promises of addiction. But her addiction only causes her more pain and destroys the potential for healing relationships. Addiction pushes her even further into darkness, and she continues to stumble down the road to destruction.

WHY WE CHOOSE THE
Road to Destruction

The road to destruction is a broad one. There's room on it for many addictions, and they come in many forms. The most common addictions I've seen among survivors involve sex, drugs and alcohol, food, and self-injury. The one thing that they have in common is that while we choose them because they seem to be ways to cope with abuse, they all leave us worse off than we started.

Sexual addiction is a common outcome of abuse in childhood. Like Noelle, children who have been victims of sexual abuse can grow up confusing sex with love or believing that sex is the only way they can relate to others. For such people, sex is a sad substitute for a healing circle.

One form of sexual addiction is masturbation. As a young girl, Kelsie's own father sexually abused her. Her body was awakened to sexual touch at an early age, and she grew up masturbating at night in bed. Now as an adult, Kelsie is addicted. Masturbation has become a destructive cycle of shame and isolation that causes her to withdraw from relationships.

Pornography is another form of sexual addiction, one that is taking a huge toll on relationships as it rips to shreds the lives of individuals, families, and churches. Lee was seven when his babysitter first showed him pornographic pictures on the Internet. After a few weeks of looking at these images together, the babysitter began kissing and fondling Lee. Eventually he raped him. Lee was afraid to tell, so he never did, and as a teen, he continued to look at porn on his own. As he searched for increasingly graphic and degrading material, he isolated himself from relationships. He needed help, but he shut out the people who could have supported him. Eventually none of the images he could find excited him anymore, and in the end, he acted out his sick fantasies the same way his babysitter once had—by raping a child.

One of the most common destroyers of relationships is addiction to drugs or alcohol. Sharon's husband, Darryl, is a survivor of childhood sexual abuse. In an e-mail to me about Darryl's drug use, Sharon told me that it had developed after the death of his abuser. She said that Darryl wouldn't talk about his feelings and denied that he was addicted. She felt helpless as he turned to drugs instead of to her. She felt that all she could do was watch as their family began to crumble.

Marcus had a big brother whose friends would come over to

his house in the summer while his parents were at work. At first Marcus thought it was cool that they would take him to the park and allow him to hang out with them. But that didn't last long. Soon when he heard they were coming over, he would hide in the basement. When they found him, they would force him to take shots of liquor until he passed out and then gang-rape him.

ONE OF THE most common destroyers of relationships is addiction to drugs or alcohol.

Until I spoke at the university Marcus attended, although years had passed since those horrendous events, he had never told anyone about them. While we were talking, I stressed how important it was for him to surround himself with a circle of inspiration and in that safe place talk about what he had gone through.

"I don't need anyone," he replied. "Alcohol got me through it then and it will get me through it now." He said he would rather get drunk and forget than talk and remember.

But as Marcus continued to talk to me, he began to cry. Deep down he wanted healthy relationships and a better life. Yes, drinking had numbed him and gotten him through to that point, but now he wanted freedom. He wanted healing. And he knew that his addiction was keeping him from finding both. He knew there was a better road; he had just never been able to find it on his own.

I have talked with countless survivors who use food to cope with abuse. Compulsive overeating or binge eating seem to be a way to fill the lonely void they feel inside. Eve says, "Food is my friend. Food doesn't say hurtful things, and it doesn't run away when I get close. Food keeps my attention when I don't want to think about anything else and comforts me when I'm down."

Sometimes overeating is a way to create a physical barrier between ourselves and others. Candi believed the lie that she was raped because she was attractive. Subconsciously, she decided that being overweight would make her unattractive and thus keep her safe from another assault. As a result, she became a food addict.

Bulimia and anorexia are also addictive responses to abuse. For some victims, vomiting is a way to rid themselves of the feeling of shame that abuse has caused. When used as a form of self-punishment, starving oneself ultimately leads to suicide. All food-related addictions keep survivors from forming the supportive relationships they so desperately need.

Self-injury, or SI, is an alarming trend that I've found in most every city, town, community, church youth group, college, and school I've visited. I've spent time talking and praying with many who share with me their stories (and sometimes their scars) of cutting, burning, biting, and beating themselves, or pulling out their hair. If there's one thing that hurts my heart the most, it is knowing how many people, silently hurting from the pain of sexual abuse, are punishing their own bodies for something they didn't deserve to begin with.

While she was growing up, Erykah was a victim of an alcoholic and abusive father. As an adult, she found herself in a destructive pattern of dating men who were as violent as he was. At twenty-one she had bruises on both her body and her spirit. And when an abusive partner wasn't around, she would injure herself. Cutting herself or hitting her head against a wall eased her feelings of loneliness, sadness, and shame—at least for the moment. Erykah was looking for a circle of inspiration, but because of her low view of herself, what she found was a cycle of violence.

Besides the addictions I've mentioned, there are many other ways of coping that can set survivors on the road to destruction. Maybe your way isn't what most people would even consider an addiction. Maybe it's something much less dramatic. My substitute was to fill my life with activities, hobbies, achievements, and work. I know that throughout my childhood and well into my teens I did this as a way to escape painful memories. With such a busy life, I didn't have time to think about the suffering going on inside or the need to spend time with my circle of inspiration.

Behind all of these unhealthy responses to abuse I see a distinct pattern: a need for control. Many survivors with eating disorders tell me that for the first time in their lives, they feel as if they have control over something—food. They think that if they can control their pain, they'll feel better and safer. But it never works. Being skinny or overweight doesn't protect us from being wounded again. Overeating or vomiting never make our problems go away. Satan wants us to believe that we are powerful if we can choose to overeat or not eat—or to drink, use drugs, hurt ourselves, have sex, or look at pornographic images—but the irony is that the thing that we think we can control will eventually control us. Second Peter 2:19 says that we are slaves to whatever controls us.

Trying to gain control through an addiction is just wasted energy on a path to further isolation and eventual destruction. It can help you flee reality and deaden your painful memories for a while, but the numbing sensation won't last forever. The addiction will not only grow worse and worse, but it will also take a huge toll on the relationships you do have. How much better it would be to use that energy to take steps forward on the road to healing!

I understand the many reasons survivors resort to an addiction as a substitute for a circle of inspiration, and I know that many of you may be using any number of them as a way to survive. I get that. However, I also know that there's a better way, and I want you to know it too. You deserve to walk the right road, the road of healing and freedom and life.

HELPING A SURVIVOR FIND
the Road of Life

If you know someone who is struggling with an addiction, I want to encourage you to support him. This will require a lot of understanding and patience on your part. Sometimes you may feel as if the relationship goes only one way and that you aren't getting anything in return. That can be frustrating, and you may even get hurt in the process. But please don't give up.

Most survivors don't really want to hurt themselves. It's just something that has "worked" for them. Most likely the survivor you want so desperately to help has convinced himself that his addiction is the only thing that will take away his pain. Remember that from his perspective, his addiction is what has enabled him to endure the very worst of situations. You can be the one to show him that he has better options.

I once heard someone say that when we focus on the problem, we can't see the solution. I agree with that. An addicted survivor who continually stares at the hole within himself will never look up to see the One who can fill it. As a member of his circle of inspiration, you can be the one to show him that while he can choose to focus on either the problem or the solution, only God has the power to set him free. That's what Shawn learned when he allowed others to come alongside and support him in his struggle with sexual addiction.

When Shawn was willing to be honest with himself about his sexual sin and his need for healing from past sexual abuse, God led him to a support group. Shawn began by seeing a Christian counselor. "During that first session," he says, "my counselor asked if I had any struggles with pornography or masturbation. When I said that I was currently struggling with an addiction to masturbation, he recommended that I attend a Christian men's support group for sexual addiction. I knew that if I was really serious about healing, I needed to do this, even though I don't like going to new places alone to meet with strangers. God gave me the courage to step out in faith, and for the first time I told a group of strangers about my past sexual abuse and my sexual struggles.

"It turned out that those strangers weren't so strange after all. For the very first time, I felt accepted for who I was, including my struggle with sexual sin. I had a sense of freedom just knowing that I wasn't alone in my struggle. It wasn't long before I had many loving and caring friends walking with me through my suffering. Through them, God has delivered me from sexual addiction as He has continued to heal me."

Our own willpower isn't enough. Relying on our ability to say no will only mean more lost battles, more shame, and more pain. If we could rescue ourselves, we wouldn't need a Savior. He is the only One who can rescue us and keep us on the right road.

Most of us don't come to this path-changing realization on our own, especially if we are blinded by our addiction. We need the light of God shining through others to help us find the way. That's what Maya's friend and mentor did for her. "She helped me see that I had to stop putting my energy into my addiction and to give it to the Lord," Maya said. "I had to replace one master with the other. I couldn't serve both. It's physically impossible to give your life and heart to both. No idol created by addiction can ever match God's infinite power to meet the human need for safety and security. I've found that He is the only thing that satisfies." Like Maya, all survivors need people around them to shed light into their dark corner and help them find the road to life.

Survivors are often afraid to confront addictions for fear of what other people will think. Their means of coping have worked for them, and they don't see any reason to expose something so shameful. So the addiction continues to grow, and the more they go back to it, the more it eats away at their sense of identity and hope.

We're all partly to blame for this. We've numbed ourselves to the prevalence of sexual abuse and totally rejected the fact that we could just as easily be in a survivor's shoes, walking the road of addiction. We see ourselves as better than others who struggle with this or that, because we think that our own shortcomings aren't as bad. But the truth is that all sin is the same. None is worse than any other. Who are we to pass judgment? We're all human and all capable of falling into addiction. Acknowledging this is critical to helping a survivor find his way off of the destructive road and onto the right road.

Remember that none of us is ever defined by what we have gone through in the past or what we are going through now. We can say that it happened to us, that it has affected us, and that we're struggling with it, but that isn't the same as being defined by it. A survivor is not his eating disorder, his drug of choice, or his sexual addiction. He doesn't have to be enslaved to it, and through Christ and with your help as a member of his circle of inspiration, he can overcome it.

Paul wrote: "The temptations in your life are no different from what others experience. And God is faithful. He will not allow the temptation to be more than you can stand. When you are tempted, he will show you a way out so that you can endure" (1 Corinthians 10:13). I believe that when the pull of addiction and the temptation to walk the road of death is strong, this verse will bring power into a survivor's circumstances. Encourage her to speak it aloud and to look for the way out. It's always there. And the more she chooses the road of life, the easier it will be for her to reject the lies coming from the road of destruction.

Betsy struggled with self-injury for a few years. But once she told her secret and began her healing journey, she found the support she needed to say no to her urges once in a while. When she replaced her addiction with a circle of inspiration, she found that she could do something different than she would usually do because she had the help she needed. What an amazing testimony to have control over the thing that once controlled her!

THE REST of the Story

While Jesus was busy writing in the dust, the scribes and Pharisees kept demanding that He answer their question. They weren't interested in what He was writing in the dirt. They weren't interested in justice. And they certainly weren't interested in finding out why the woman had taken the wrong road or in helping her find the right one. They were focused on only one thing. They wanted Jesus to answer their question: Should the woman caught in the act of adultery be stoned, or shouldn't she?

"So he stood up again and said, 'All right, but let the one who has never sinned throw the first stone!' Then he stooped down again and wrote in the dust.

"When the accusers heard this, they slipped away one by one, beginning with the oldest, until only Jesus was left in the middle of the crowd with the woman.

"Then Jesus stood up again and said to the woman, 'Where are your accusers? Didn't even one of them condemn you?'

"'No, Lord,' she said.

"And Jesus said, 'Neither do I. Go and sin no more.'" (John 8: 7–11).

Jesus wasn't saying that the woman hadn't sinned. He knew she had, and everybody else knew it too. What He was saying was that He didn't condemn her. In saying that, He was also claiming to be God, for God is the only one qualified to condemn anyone. The Jewish religious leaders slunk away because they knew that their own sins made them as guilty as the woman was.

As imperfect, fallible human beings, we never have the right to condemn anyone. Whenever we point a finger at someone else, there are three fingers pointing back at us. Inappropriate sexual behavior is often an indication of brokenness or a deeply felt need for intimacy or relationship. People who choose to walk that road—or any other road of addiction—don't deserve our scorn or condemnation. They deserve our compassion, our commitment to their healing, and our help in finding the road of life.

In the next verse, Jesus makes it clear how we can step off the dark road that leads to destruction. "I am the light of the world. If you follow me, you won't have to walk in darkness, because you will have the light that leads to life'" (v.12). To walk the path to life, we must follow Jesus.

A Life Letter

Dear Fellow Survivor . . .

As a rape survivor, I used to have painful emotions that I didn't know how to handle in a healthy way. In an attempt to rid myself of the pain, I began to take pills to numb my body. I lived for that high, when everything seemed to be okay and I could no longer feel the sting of what had happened to me. But the numbing effect lasted only a short time, and after the high ended, I always turned back to the pills.

My attempt to numb my pain only led me down the path to more destruction. I found myself doing it over and over again until there came a time when I held an entire bottle of pills in my hand, wanting to end my own life. I remember my hands shaking as I held them, wondering how the very thing that was supposed to help me had become my chosen means of suicide.

It was then that I realized that I wasn't meant to take this journey by myself. I had to tell others the truth about my addiction and the root of it, my rape, before any type of healing could ever occur. It wasn't until I learned to accept help that I began to walk down the path leading to freedom.

It's easy for us to conclude that no one can possibly help us, not even God Himself. Satan wants you to believe this lie. He knows we need people to help get us through our pain, so he makes addiction appear as a form of support to isolate us from real help and healing. What we fail to recognize is that we are not alone. God not only offers His loving support, but also support through those He places around us.

First, I had to go to the Lord, the ultimate source of comfort, truth, and love. I also had to open up to my church body and others around me. Initially, I had many fears about revealing my shame to people, but once I did, I learned that it was well worth it. They provided me with accountability, encouragement, and hope. They fixed my eyes on Jesus when all that I could seem to see was my own pain. Without them, I would still be turning to pills. When I reached out for others, I learned that they were also reaching out to me. Allowing them to take my hand helped me get through some of the darkest and most painful times in my life.

It's impossible to face the pain of abuse and addiction on our own, but when we let God and others be our support, the journey doesn't look so terrifying. What looks impossible to the human eye is nothing in the eyes of Almighty God. No matter how awful our circumstances may have become, He is always there to provide us with a healthy circle: a place of truth where others will stand by us and battle our pain with us.

Letting go of my addiction and holding on to the Lord and those He had given me helped me reach my goal: freedom. By God's grace and my supportive circle, I am now free of addiction and of the haunting memories of my past. The amazing thing is that God has used my freedom to inspire others to find freedom from their own addictions. He has brought people to me who were in similar circumstances so that I could comfort them the way He comforted me. Just as He has done with me, the Lord is waiting to use you in the lives of others. Reach out to those around you with the same love and support that you have always looked for.

—Yolanda

Part Two
INHALING

Flavia is one of my favorite artists, and I have one of her pieces hanging in my home. The caption reads: "Some people come into our lives and quickly go. Some stay for a while, leave footprints on our hearts, and we are never, ever the same." This reminds me of the kind of relationships I have experienced on my healing journey.

I have an amazing circle of inspiration made up of family, a spouse, friends, a church body, and most importantly, the Lord. I know the inspirational role each one of them has played in my healing and will continue to play as I keep moving forward on this lifelong journey toward wholeness.

Each has been much more than just a spectator who has cheered me on from the sidelines as I've made my way down the dark tunnel of healing. Yes, they have done that. But they have done much more. Some have held out a cup of water, some have given me a push when I've lost my motivation, some have carried me when I've needed to rest, and some have held a flashlight to light the path when the next step has seemed too dark or scary. All have in some way breathed new life into me on my healing journey.

Though they have played many different roles, each member of my circle has left a lasting footprint on my path of healing as well as on my heart. Because of them, I have been free to breathe.

4

FAMILY
Matters

Family Matters Family Matters Family Matters Family Matters Family Matters Matters Matters

THOUGH MY FATHER AND MOTHER FORSAKE ME, THE LORD WILL RECEIVE ME.

—Psalm 27:10 NIV

A family's response to the sexual abuse of one of its own is critical for the victim's healing. To her, family matters the most. While you may think that a victim's parents and siblings would be the ones most likely to breathe new life into her, sadly, they're often the very ones that suck the life right out of her. This happens not only when a family member is responsible for the abuse, but also when others in the family tell the victim to *hush*. The Bible tells the story of a family in which both of these things occurred.

This didn't happen in just any old family. It happened in a family where you would least expect it—the family of King David, "a man after God's own heart." Since the victim, Tamar, is the only daughter of King David mentioned in Scripture, God clearly wants us to learn something from her story. Otherwise it would never have been recorded. So let's take a close look at Tamar's story to see what God has to say about how her family deprived her of justice and doomed her to a desolate existence by the unloving way they responded to her abuse.

SOMEONE WHO NEEDED
a Loving Response

In 2 Samuel, we learn that Tamar was a beautiful virgin and that her half-brother Amnon became obsessed with having her. Acting on the advice of his cousin, Amnon took to his bed and acted sick. "When the king came to see him, Amnon asked him, 'Please let my sister Tamar come and cook my favorite dish as I watch. Then I can eat it from her own hands.' So David agreed and sent Tamar to

Amnon's house to prepare some food for him" (13:6–7).

Tamar was an innocent young woman who was full of compassion for others. She loved her half-brother, trusted him, and respected him as the heir to their father's throne. So when her father told her to go help Amnon, she went without a second thought.

Tamar made the dish Amnon had requested, but he refused to eat. Instead, he sent everybody else out of the room and asked her to bring the food to his bed and feed it to him herself. Still suspecting nothing, she complied, whereupon he grabbed her. Using the only weapon she had—her voice—Tamar tried to reason with Amnon.

In his lust, Amnon refused to listen. Instead, he overpowered Tamar and raped her. Then he told her to get up and get out. Bruised and bleeding, Tamar still attempted to reason with him. "'No!' she said to him. 'Sending me away would be a greater wrong than what you have already done to me'" (v.16 NIV). She was ashamed to go outside, for she knew what others would think of her. Again, Amnon refused to listen. He called his servant and had him throw Tamar out on the street. Weeping loudly, she made her way home.

CAN YOU RELATE?

In some ways, it's easy for me to relate to Tamar. As a young girl, I grew up in a small town—you know, one of those places where everybody knows everybody. Like Tamar, I seemed to have the perfect life. I was very involved in school and sports. I was popular and had tons of friends. But at the same time, I was a hurting little girl, miserable and scared, wishing I were someone else, planning how to run away, and fantasizing about my own funeral.

Why would a little girl who had so much going for her be in so much pain? Because I carried a deep, dark secret: my very own stepfather—a man I loved and trusted, a man who was respected in our community—was sexually abusing me.

Unlike Tamar, I was too young to reason with my abuser. In fact, I was too young to even know for sure that what he was doing was wrong. He told me it was normal; I loved him and trusted what he said. I thought that there was something wrong with me. I was also afraid to tell anyone what my stepfather was doing because he said that no one would believe me. And he always told me that it if I did tell, the police would take me away from my mom and make me live with someone else. At that point, my future, like Tamar's, looked very bleak.

What about Tamar's siblings and parents? How did they react to their daughter's abuse?

Most likely, the news reached home before Tamar did, for when she arrived, the first thing her brother Absalom asked her was "Has your brother Amnon had his way with you?" When Tamar told her brother what had happened, he gave her the same horrible advice that people often give someone in their family who has been sexually abused: "'Now, my dear sister, let's keep it quiet—a family matter. He is, after all, your brother. Don't take this so hard'" (2 Samuel 13:20 *The Message*).

Although Scripture tells us nothing about Tamar's mother, it says that when King David heard about the rape, he was furious. That's all. He was angry, but he did nothing. As the father of both the guilty party and the victim, David was responsible for punishing Amnon. As the king, he was responsible for ensuring that justice was done. But he did neither. The bottom line is that David failed Tamar miserably. There was no punishment, no justice.

The message Tamar's family sent her was "*Hush!* Stuff your feelings, bury the hurt, and try to forget about it. For the sake of the family, don't talk about it." That's when Tamar lost her voice. In following the family rules, she condemned herself to a life of silence, solitude, and sorrow.

While Tamar lost her voice because her family failed her, I eventually found mine because my mother did not fail me. At fourteen, I finally found the courage to tell her, and when I did, she didn't tell me to *hush*. Instead, she believed me and reported the abuse to Children's Services. We were in hiding for nearly a week, fearing for our lives if my stepfather found us. Seven days later, he committed suicide.

The death of my stepfather brought me freedom, but it didn't bring me peace. Even though I would no longer experience sexual abuse, like Tamar, I was left with the humiliation and devastation that my abuser's sin had caused. I felt alone, dirty, damaged, and ashamed. I felt as if everything was my fault, and I was afraid of what other people would think of me if they knew the truth. I vowed to never reveal my secret to anyone else and to try to block it out of my mind and move on. I was on my way to becoming a desolate woman. Thankfully, a few years later I decided to take the next step on my healing journey.

WHY WE SHUT OUT
Our Family

Although you'd think that family members would be the first ones a survivor would turn to for protection, understanding, and help, they are often the last. There are three basic reasons for this.

The first reason is our feelings of fear. We can be afraid to talk to members of our family about the abuse because our abuser always told us to keep it a secret and we fear the consequences if we do talk to them about it. Abusers use many fear tactics to keep their victims silent. I was afraid no one would believe me. I was afraid I would be hurt even more, or that someone I cared about would be hurt. Even after my secret was out, I was afraid of what my mom would think of me if she knew how the abuse was affecting me. I was afraid of losing her, which was exactly what my stepfather had always told me would happen if I told. I was also afraid of telling her too much because I didn't want to overwhelm her or add to her own pain.

Hartley was afraid that if she shared her secret, she would ruin her family's name and they would disown her. "I was afraid to tell my family back home that I was molested as a child and that I became anorexic and a cutter in response to the abuse. I was mostly afraid because of the expectations and perceptions people had about me because I'm a PK (Preacher's Kid). I was afraid I'd ruin my family's reputation. So instead of opening up to them, I wore a mask. I pretended to be what others expected me to be: a perfect Christian girl with no problems."

Our feelings of responsibility can also interfere with having a healthy relationship with members of our family. I believed not only that the abuse was my fault, but also that it was my responsibility to keep my family together. I thought this was my burden to carry. As a teenager, I felt as though I had to protect my mom and that I was responsible for keeping her happy. This is too much for anyone to take on, no matter how old. I needed to talk about this with my mom and hear from her that I was allowed to be a teenager and to do normal things for my age. I needed her to tell me that I wasn't responsible for my abuse, for holding my family together, or for her.

When Jaimie broke the silence about being abused by her father three years earlier, her mother, Colleen, supported her. She left her husband and protected her daughter. Since then, however, Colleen has become emotionally dependent on Jaimie, and their relationship has taken an unhealthy turn. Colleen has no friends outside of her daughter and often makes Jaimie feel guilty for spending time with others.

When Jaimie graduated from high school, she felt called to attend a college that had a special program in a field she had always wanted to study. But the school was five hours away, and because of the pressure she felt to stay near her mother, she decided to go to her local community college. Feeling responsible for her mom's happiness, Jaimie gave up her own dreams and desires to meet the unhealthy emotional needs of her mother.

Colleen is unknowingly sucking the life out of Jaimie, and their relationship has suffered. While an adult child can definitely be part of her parent's support system, meeting her parent's emotional needs should never be her sole responsibility. Colleen needs to find her own support and friendships outside of her daughter. Jamie and Colleen both need to understand that they each have a separate identity. They can complement each other, but they cannot be fully responsible for each other's well-being and happiness. Jaimie has her own destiny to fulfill, and she needs the freedom to go out and find it, just as her mother does. Only then will they both find true happiness.

Finally, feelings of sadness can interfere with our relationship with our family. Having been betrayed by someone our family loved or trusted causes a great deal of sadness. I struggled in this area. I didn't want to talk to my mom about it because I didn't want her to feel guilty for not having known what was happening. But it ate away at me, and eventually we discussed it. Talking about it helped me understand that what had happened was wrong, that it wasn't my fault, and that my abuser had fooled everyone.

Rachel was afraid to tell her mother about her abuse because the man responsible was her mother's very close friend. "My abuse had ended years ago, and I hardly ever saw this man anymore, " Rachel told me. "It seemed like a bad idea to bring it up to my mom. I knew it would hurt her because she would feel as if she had been to blame for bringing him around so much."

Over time, Rachel's secret ate away at her, and she knew she needed to talk to her mom about it. "I wrote my mom a note and had her read it while I was sitting with her," she said. Rachel's mother expressed her love and concern and apologized to her daughter for what she had been through. "She wasn't mad. She was more worried about me and the fact that I had kept it in for so long. She was calm and loving and said that if I didn't want to tell the police, I didn't have to. But if I did, she would walk beside me every step of the way. She also helped me find and pay for a counselor. By telling my mom my secret, I began the healing process. I'm so relieved to not be suffering in silence anymore!"

Unfortunately, many parents of survivors are like King David was—not the most supportive. Just as damaging as the abuse itself is the unloving response of family members when they hear about it. Sadly, one of the most common stories I hear is of a victim telling a nonoffending parent or other trusted family member and being told to "hush."

It breaks my heart every time I hear this, for I know how devastating this response is to those who are broken, hurting, and vulnerable. Not only is it an incredible letdown for the victim, but it plants lies in his mind: "I must be bad"; "It was my fault"; "No one cares"; "I am dirty and everyone thinks so"; "I should have kept it a secret." Lies like these, confirmed by a family member's initial response to the revelation, can set a victim on the path to desolation.

Families who don't even acknowledge that any abuse has occurred can be just as damaging. If this is your situation, remember that you get to choose who is in your circle of inspiration. This is your circle. It's your team, and you are the captain. Only those who acknowledge the abuse and are willing to walk with you on the path ahead are allowed in. You have the right to exclude anyone—even a parent—who is unwilling to admit that you have been wronged. You can still heal without the support of your family. Even if your family can't help breathe life into you, God is able.

However, if you do have family members who want to help you heal, I encourage you to include them in your circle. This is a very important relationship in your life, and having family members in your circle can greatly enhance the healing process by reassuring you of the truth about the abuse, about yourself, and about their love for you. This is especially true of parents.

MAKING A DIFFERENCE AS A PARENT

Recently I received a letter from Mandi telling me how she responded when she learned that her young daughter, Bristin, had been abused. As I read, it struck me that Mandi did the most important things she needed to do as a parent to protect and support her child.

"When Bristin was six years old," Mandi said, "a man who lived next door to her best friend was convicted of sexually molesting a minor and put in jail. After this happened, I talked with Bristin about inappropriate touching. At the time, she didn't say much. However, the next week, out of the blue, she came to me and said, 'Mommy, Jeremy touches me like that.'

CHILDREN need to know they have a voice.

"I couldn't believe my ears. Jeremy was her twenty-year-old cousin, whom she loved deeply. He may have been goofy, playful, and immature, but surely he wasn't a sexual predator! I didn't want her to overreact to kind and playful gestures from loving family members. So as I talked with Bristin, I told her that not every touch is a bad touch. I dismissed it as a misunderstanding.

"However, a few days later Bristin approached me again and said the same thing. Only this time she asked me to lie on the couch on my stomach so she could show me what happened. She then proceeded to climb onto my back and rub roughly back and forth. I knew without a shadow of a doubt that she was telling the truth."

Mandi let her daughter know at an early age that it was not okay for anyone to touch her in an inappropriate way and that she could talk to her about it if anyone ever did. She made sure that Bristin could talk to her about anything that made her feel uncomfortable, and when she did talk about it, Mandi believed her. In this way, Mandi established an open relationship with her daughter that validated her worth and gave her an incredible sense of security, a basic need of all children.

Children need to know they have a voice. Assure them of their right to say no to uncomfortable situations. Forcing a child to sit on Grandpa's lap denies her the right to say no to something that might feel unsafe. Allowing her to make decisions in circumstances like this gives her a feeling of ownership of her body and can help protect her in a potentially harmful situation. Talk with her later about her decision to not sit in Grandpa's lap. Maybe she simply didn't feel like reading a story with Grandpa, and that's okay, but maybe there's something deeper. If there is, you've given her a voice that can alert you that something may be wrong and thus possibly prevent abuse from occurring.

You also need to pay attention to signs that something is amiss: stomachaches, headaches, urinary tract infections, knowledge of sexual things at an age that doesn't make sense, outbursts of anger, nightmares, fear of certain people, anxiety, and bed-wetting, to name a few.

"In hindsight," Mandi said, "I realized that I had missed important signs that Bristin was being abused. She had suffered from stomachaches for no apparent reason. She had also had some anxiety attacks that were out of character for her. She would have fits of rage at the rest of the family. All of these things occurred over a period of time before we knew what was going on. In counseling, we learned that these are classic signs of a loss of control, which she was experiencing because of the abuse."

Kids often hint that something is wrong and making them feel uncomfortable. If you notice anything out of character for your child, ask questions, even if it's difficult for you. Kids don't make up this stuff, and if they feel safe with you, they will talk. If they do tell you that something has happened, try to stay calm for their sake. "I was very calm around Bristin," Mandi said, "even though I was shaking on the inside. I told her that I was so proud of her for telling me and that she had done nothing wrong."

Be loving, accepting, kindhearted, reassuring, and protective. Tell your child that what happened to him was wrong and that he didn't deserve it. Let him know over and over that it wasn't his fault. Thank him for telling you about it and tell him that it took a great deal of courage for him to do that. Let him know you will do all you can to protect him and help him heal as he is ready.

"We reported the abuse to the authorities and immediately got Bristin into counseling," Mandi said. "Both a detective and a children's service worker met with Bristin, my husband, and me. Bristin's story never changed, and her counseling sessions went very well." Mandi says that Bristin rarely mentions her abuse now. But when she does, Mandi stops and listens to her daughter and tries to help her work it out a little bit more. She follows her daughter's lead.

Remember that healing is a lifelong journey and that there will be hills and valleys along the way. It's difficult sometimes, but it will get better. Let your child know that he can talk about it whenever and to whomever he wishes. He needs to know that what happened to him is not something to be ashamed of, because he has done nothing wrong.

He needs to know that you don't look at him any differently and that your greatest concern is his safety and well-being.

Erin says that if she had to choose one person who has helped her the most, it would be her mom. "I will always remember the look on her face the day I told her that I had been abused. But she never pushed for the story. She just made sure I knew that I could talk to her when I wanted to. That was six years ago, and after becoming an alcoholic trying to deal with the abuse on my own, I finally found myself talking to my mom again. It's great to know that I can always talk to her and that if I ask her not to say anything, she won't. If I don't want to talk, I can just sit and cry, and she doesn't think any less of me. It's hard to find that anywhere else."

Make time to relate one-on-one to your child. I realize that as a parent, your schedule is probably crazy and that you may not always have time to spend just hanging out with her. But I also know that she needs you to give her your time and your undivided attention. A day or an hour, whatever she needs. A survivor of sexual abuse definitely needs this. Her love tank has been sucked dry, and a parent should be the first person to come running to fill it. Nothing is more precious to her than your time. It breathes the words "I am important" into her gasping lungs.

I know I say this all the time, but here we go again: Talking is so important! Survivors need your time and they need to talk. I can still remember some conversations I had with my mom while I was in high school. They occurred at times when I needed to process how I felt about something that had happened to me. Mom was struggling to heal from this trauma too, but she was never so self-consumed that she wasn't available to me.

Kids also need to know that it's okay if there are some things they don't want to share with their parents. Sometimes I didn't want to burden my mom with too much information when she was already dealing with a lot. Other times, I just didn't want her to be the only person I talked to. Mom never made me feel bad for wanting to talk to someone besides her. She would make sure everything was okay between us, but once she knew that it was, she gave me the freedom to go to others in my circle. That was incredibly freeing.

My father sent me the same message. One day when he was driving me to his house for the weekend, he said, "Nicole, I want you to know that I'm here if you ever want to talk about what happened with your stepdad. But if you don't ever want to talk with me about it, that's okay, too." My father's words meant so much to me then, and they still do.

Many sexual molestation cases occur in family situations, even in Christian households like Mandi's. This is a sin that reaches everywhere and destroys all the relationships in its path. Jeremy's abuse of Bristin has taken a serious toll on the relationships in their extended family.

"The family get-togethers are strained and very different now," Mandi says. "We haven't seen Jeremy since we found out, and that's sad because we still love him, but a tie has been severed. Through the power of the Holy Spirit, we can forgive, but sin has consequences, and we feel that for Bristin's sake there has to be separation. Until she is old enough to handle the stress, she needs to feel safe, which means not putting her in that situation. We take one day at a time and trust that God will work it out in His time. Meanwhile, our job is to be the best parents we can be for our daughter."

I'm convinced that with the help of God and a circle of inspiration, Mandi, Bristin, and her family will reach the light at the end of the tunnel on their healing journey.

THE REST of the Story

In one lustful act, Amnon had stripped Tamar of her dignity and destroyed her future. She was no longer a virgin, which in that culture meant that she could never marry or bear children. For a woman in Israel, that was a fate worse than death. One act of sexual violence, combined with the unloving response of family members who should have comforted and supported her, made Tamar a desolate woman. The last thing we hear about her in Scripture is that she "lived as a desolate woman in her brother Absalom's house" (2 Samuel 13:20 *The Message*).

While we don't know to what degree Tamar recovered over time, the Bible makes it clear that God did not forget her. By including her story in His Word, he gave Tamar the voice her family had denied her and vindicated her to all generations. God doesn't forget the Tamars of this world. He saw what happened to Tamar and He cared. Scripture doesn't minimize her suffering.

If you have suffered, God doesn't minimize your suffering, either. He longs to heal you and make you whole again. No matter the circumstances of your life, no matter where you have been or what you have done or what has been done to you, God loves you and promises to use everything in your life for good. He calls you His beautiful child, and He longs to make your life story beautiful as well.

Unlike Tamar's earthly father, our heavenly Father is concerned with justice. Martin Luther King Jr. once said, "Justice at its best is love correcting all that stands against love." I see sexual abuse as the ultimate expression of the lust and violence that stand against what God intended to be love. But as Dr. King said, it can be corrected. By love. Real love. Genuine love. Unconditional love. Love is the answer. Those who refuse to love us pollute our air, but those who choose to love us purify it. They inspire us to love in return, and this enables us to heal more quickly.

A Life Letter

Dear Parent . . .

As Nicole's mom, it's amazing to reflect back on the impact of just one of our many mother-daughter conversations—the one in which Nicole confided in me that my husband had been sexually abusing her.

That was the worst thing I could ever imagine happening to my daughter, to me, to our family. I couldn't understand how it could happen in my home. I was a stay-at-home mom with a home business, and I was there almost all the time. My husband loved us, and I trusted him. This was unbelievable! Yet, there it was. It had happened, and I had no problem believing it.

People often ask me, "Why did you believe her?" My answer is simple. I had no reason not to. Why would she lie about something so shameful, so degrading, so embarrassing? I'm sure there was a part of me that didn't want to believe it and that wished it would all go away, but I never doubted that Nicole had told me the truth.

Sexual abuse affects everyone in the victim's family. The power games, the manipulation, the lies, and the deceit that abusers use to cover up their crime allow evil to permeate and slowly suffocate everyone in the home. It's a blinding darkness. By telling me about the abuse, Nicole became a source of truth and light that lifted the cloak of darkness that had settled over our home. I could not live with myself today if I had turned my back on the truth.

People also ask me why I left my husband and reported the abuse. To my mind, it was the only right thing to do. Even though he was my husband and I loved him, there was never any doubt in my mind that he should be held accountable for the crime he had committed against Nicole. It was my responsibility as a mother to let my daughter know that he was the one who had done something wrong—that it was not her fault! And if I had to do it over again, I would do exactly what I did then to protect my daughter. I had to do it. What my husband had done left me with no choice.

I had no idea how much my response to Nicole during that one conversation would change our lives. As she and I have walked the healing path together, God has been faithful to take all the brokenness of our lives and to work all things together for good (Romans 8:28). He has healed us and is still healing us.

Nearly every day, Nicole meets survivors of sexual abuse who have made themselves vulnerable by telling a parent the hardest thing they could ever say: "I have been sexually abused." The majority of these victims open themselves up only to be shut down. The very person they entrust with their secret accuses them of making up stories and tells them to *hush*, leaving them afraid to ever tell anyone again.

If you have a child who someday tells you that she has been sexually abused, I pray that you will have the courage to be different. Please, please, believe her! That's the very first step in walking with her on her journey to healing. If you suspect that she is being or has been abused, provide a safe place where she can confide in you, no matter how young or how old she is. You may think that you're not capable of handling such a tremendous task, but remember this: the most important thing you have to give her is your two ears, your heart, and your time. Listen and hurt along with her. Never stop believing her, and never stop praying for her!

—Cindy

5

THE NEXT Generation

The Next Generation *The Next Generation The Next Generation The Next Generation Generation*

CHOOSE LIFE, SO THAT YOU AND YOUR CHILDREN MAY LIVE.

—Deuteronomy 30:19 NIV

What happened in King David's family was the result of his own moral failings. Although he confessed his sin of committing adultery with Bathsheba and then having her husband killed, he still abdicated his responsibility as a father and a king. As a result, he unintentionally passed down a pattern of sexual sin and violence to the next generation. The history of his family is a good example of the enduring consequences of what the Bible calls "the sins of the fathers."

This is often the kind of legacy that survivors of childhood sexual abuse unintentionally pass on to their own children. They dream of making a better life for their kids than they themselves have had. They want to meet all their children's needs in a way that allows them to develop to their full God-given potential. However, if the unhealed effects of sexual abuse have prevented them from meeting their own needs, this dream can turn into a nightmare.

Just as children are more vulnerable than adults to the harmful effects of secondhand smoke, they are also more vulnerable to the effects of an environment polluted by the effects of the abuse their parent suffered as a child. If we want our children to develop to their full potential, we must choose to deal with the toxic effects that the evil actions of others have had on our own life. Those of us who choose to become healthy ourselves are not only protecting our children's health, but also setting an example that will last for generations to come. We need to choose life so that our children may live.

When King Ahab was king of Israel, he rejected God in favor of Baal and other heathen gods. So God sent his prophet Elijah to deliver a message to the king: "'As surely as the Lord, the God of Israel, lives—the God I serve—there will be no dew or rain during the next few years until I give the word!'" (1 Kings 17:1).

After Elijah delivered his message to Ahab, God told him to hide east of the Jordan by the brook Kerith. There God took care of him. When the brook eventually dried up, God said to Elijah, "'Go and live in the village of Zarephath, near the city of Sidon. I have instructed a widow there to feed you'" (v. 9).

Zarephath was a small town north of Israel, deep in Baal-worship territory. To even get there, Elijah had to make a long, risky journey on foot through dangerous country. Despite the risks involved, Elijah immediately obeyed. When he arrived at the town and saw a woman gathering sticks, he knew that this was the widow to whom God had sent him, and he asked her to bring him a little water. As she was going to get it, he called to her to ask her to bring him a bite of bread as well.

Because of the drought, the widow could no longer provide for her or her son's own basic needs, much less those of a stranger. She and her son were among the many innocent people who were suffering as a consequence of the evil actions of King Ahab. Although they weren't connected to him in any way, they had to suffer because of him. The widow knew that she and her son were only one meal away from starvation. In fact, she was in the process of preparing their last supper when Elijah arrived.

We don't know whether the widow considered Elijah a prophet or a fool, but we do know that she had nothing to lose by doing what he asked. If she held on to the food for a final meal, it would only prolong the inevitable. But if Elijah was truly a prophet and she did what he asked, there was a chance that they would live. The choice was between certain death and the possibility of life. What would she do? What would her son have wanted her to do?

CAN YOU RELATE?

When she was a child, various men in Jean's family and neighborhood sexually abused her. As an adult, she accepted her abuse as "the way it was" and rarely spoke about it. Instead, she looked for something or someone to ease the pain she felt inside. Jumping from relationship to relationship, Jean soon had a daughter, Clara.

The effects of sexual abuse didn't end when Jean's abuse ended. Her emotional highs and lows, traumatic memories, triggers, feelings of low self-worth, fear of trusting others, and all the other common effects of childhood sexual abuse created a toxic atmosphere that hurt her daughter. Feeling suffocated herself, she couldn't give Clara the life-giving oxygen she needed. Instead, Clara inhaled the deadly fumes that seeped out of her mother's unhealed trauma.

Because Jean wasn't willing to address the issues in her own life that were keeping her in a cycle of unhealthy relationships, she unwittingly created a toxic environment that put her daughter at risk. Though Jean was single throughout Clara's childhood, there was always a man in their home, and Jean had no idea that many of them molested her own daughter. Like the widow of Zarephath and her son, Clara was a victim of evil that was passed down from others.

WHY IT CAN BE HARD
to Choose Life

As a child, I had no way of knowing that sexual abuse, denial, and addiction had been in my family for generations. Just as no one would have suspected that I had been a victim of sexual abuse, I would never have guessed that my own mother had been a victim as well. When you read the "life letter" at the end of chapter 1, I bet it didn't even cross your mind that the true author was my mother. For her, getting real began by realizing that what happened to me was sexual abuse. This was the key to her recognizing abuse for what it was in her own childhood.

Not long after I told my secret to my mother, she briefly shared her own secret with me. A few years later, I found Mom in the guest bedroom, where she often prayed and spent time with the Lord.

She was lying on the bed with her Bible and prayer journal, crying into a pillow. I asked her if she was okay. She was sobbing so hard that she could barely speak, but she asked me to hug her, and I did. I sat on the bed with her and held her as her sobbing subsided and she slowly read to me from that day's journal entry the details of a memory she had held inside for many years.

In some ways, Mom was like the widow of Zarephath. What both needed to do was to look to God and let Him meet their needs. But because of the unacknowledged trauma and pain from her childhood, my mom grew up choosing to look to others to meet her many needs, which caused her even more hurt and pain as a young adult. Only in the darkest and lowest point in our lives did Mom come to see the light and realize that depending on the Lord was the only answer. And thank God she came to a point of truly accepting this! Because she did, neither her life nor mine will ever be the same.

Acknowledging my abuse opened the door for Mom to acknowledge her own abuse and to begin her healing journey. It also caused us both to explore the sin and dysfunction that had occurred in our family over generations so that we could process it and thus begin to heal from it.

Abuse, along with many other signs of brokenness in families, tends to repeat itself from generation to generation. Like the Energizer Bunny, it just keeps going and going and going. When you go back and trace the path and history of family secrets, it's a no-brainer to conclude that secret sin and dysfunction will continue unless the pattern is broken. Sexual abuse survivors who become parents have the opportunity to break this cycle of generational sin. But to do this, they have to be aware of the things that stand in the way of choosing life.

The effects of abuse can cause parents to be less available to their children. Survivors experiencing depression, anxiety, guilt, shame, frustration, or rage will likely do everything they can to suppress these feelings. The problem is that when we shut off these negative emotions, we also shut off positive ones. Moms and dads need to feel. They need to be balanced and strong emotionally in order to be good parents. Working through the effects of abuse will bring emotional stability, enable kids to feel that their parents can relate to them, and set an example for them of how to cope in a healthy way with the day-to-day stresses of life.

Parents who shut off emotionally can also cause a role reversal within the parent-child relationship. As the daughter of a survivor of sexual abuse, Emma felt as if she were the parent and her mother the child. While she was growing up, she had to care for her mother, so she never received the care or attention that was vital to her own development. Forced to grow up way too fast, she missed out on the childhood she deserved to experience.

Emma and other children in similar situations feel exactly the same as their parent felt as a victim of childhood sexual abuse— that their childhood has been stolen from them. Because Emma's mother didn't acknowledge her pain and work through it, Emma grew up with her own carbon copies of the losses her mother experienced as a little girl.

Wounded parents sometimes place unrealistic expectations on their kids, pushing them to overachieve in order to overcome their own imperfect childhood. A parent who hasn't walked the road of healing can put too much pressure on his child to be what he longed to be but because of childhood abuse, never was.

Bobby's dad had dreamed of being a successful lawyer and influential leader in the community. Because he was unable to realize his own childhood dreams, he did all he could to see that they came true in the life of his son. He pushed Bobby to make perfect grades, join all the right clubs, and prepare himself to study law at a prestigious university. But Bobby's dreams weren't the same as his dad's. He was just an average student and wanted to study art, not law. Resisting the pressure to be someone he wasn't caused a strain in the father-son relationship and made Bobby feel unworthy and unloved because he wasn't able to meet his father's expectations.

Parents who were abused in childhood need to understand that their child didn't play any role in the abuse and can never do anything to fulfill the dreams that were shattered because of it. What they need to do now is to be the kind of parents who can meet their child's need for sustenance, safety, love, and self-esteem. Distant, selfish, or demanding parents aren't even able to meet their own needs, much less those of their children. Only parents who are emotionally healthy and available can meet their children's needs in a way that enables them to develop into the people God meant them to be.

When children don't know what's going on in the life of a hurting parent, they can't support him. Leaving children in the dark about these deep matters creates more confusion and chaos in the parent-child relationship and in the family circle. But if everyone is on the same page, a parent can benefit from the potential reservoir of support, encouragement, and motivation that can come from kids. Sharing your heart with your children may seem very risky, but allowing yourself to be open and vulnerable will build trust, intimacy, and the opportunity for deeper relationship and healing.

Watching my own mother cope with the ups and downs of life as she struggled through single parenthood, was healed from the effects of her abuse as well as mine, and sought the Lord in everything has had a great impact on how I live and the way I address life's issues, big and small. She allowed me to see both her strengths and weaknesses. She also communicated well with me. She never kept me in the dark about important matters. I believe this has provided the foundation for the healthy communication and great friendship I now have with her in adulthood.

When we aren't communicating with the generations following us, we're allowing generational sin to continue its cycle. I don't believe that anyone wants the sins that have devastated us to also devastate our children, but I do believe that many of us are afraid to do anything to stop it. When we are led by fear, Satan has his way.

One of the most priceless gifts we can offer our children is to trace the pattern of brokenness in our family—whether it's addiction, premarital sex, adultery, abuse, denial, or anything else—and to decide to break free of the mold so that sin won't continue its reign in their lives. We need to stand in the gap for the next generation by confessing the sins of the fathers, seeking God's forgiveness, and asking Him to bless our seed.

HELPING BREAK THE
Generational Curse

As an adult child of a sexual abuse survivor who wants to see your parent heal, you have an amazing opportunity to help him as part of his circle of inspiration. Whether you've grown up in a toxic environment or not, you can create a breathing space for him in which healing can take place. This will take a lot of understanding on your part, as unhealed childhood trauma can surface seemingly out of the blue, often years after the abuse.

Many adult survivors from all over the world tell me that they began to acknowledge what had happened to them when their own child reached the same age they were when they were abused. At Lori's tenth birthday party, her best friend's father raped her. However, Lori had no memory of what had happened to her until she began planning her own daughter's tenth birthday party, when the truth began to emerge. Her child's age and circumstances triggered the pain from her own past and opened the door for the healing that Lori needed. Oftentimes stress and burnout later in life can also cause painful childhood memories to surface. Thus, it isn't uncommon to find a survivor in his thirties and forties—or even fifties and sixties—just beginning to deal with his abuse in childhood.

In either case, you may find it very difficult to understand why your parent is just now dealing with something that happened so long ago. And if you've never been a victim of sexual abuse or been told to *hush*, you may have a hard time coming to terms with the sudden changes in your parent and the potential disruption of the entire family structure.

Understand that your parent isn't crazy. He's simply beginning to face something that he should have been free to work through years ago, but which he was forced to hide instead. Your dad needs to know that it's okay to take time off when he's burned out and needs time to heal. He needs to know that his health is more important than his career, his household chores, or his public image. Give him that space. It can be hard to see him in a different way than you're used to, but it might be exactly what he needs right now to make a big difference down the road.

Hurting people don't make the best decisions in parenting, just as they don't make the best decisions in relationships in general. What you have experienced from your mom in the past may have been a distortion of your true mother. Her wounds need to be healed in order for her to function properly. Allow the real mom to come forth. This may be difficult for you, but the results will be worth it, for in the end you'll have a much healthier, happier, and more stable mother. Pray for your parent, and ask the Lord to help you offer forgiveness if she hasn't been all she should have been for you. This will help you see through the eyes of Christ and be there for her in ways you may have never dreamed of.

You can also be a set of listening ears for your parent's spouse, whether he's your dad or a stepdad, and encourage him on this journey. Let him know that this tough time is temporary and that things will get better. Encourage him to stick it out for the reward of a healthier relationship with his wife and his entire family. Show compassion, and try not to look at him as being weak. Instead, look beyond the present circumstances to the sin that was perpetrated against his spouse. Encourage him with lovingkindness, grace, and support. Encourage him to seek counseling.

As an adult child of a sexual abuse survivor, you can help strengthen the relationship between your parents because you are in a position to see clearly the things they can provide each other. Survivors need compassion and nurturing support from their spouse, and their children are usually the best ones to encourage that.

José's stepmother was a victim of rape as a child, but she never spoke of it until a few years into her marriage to José's father, when she began seeing a counselor and attending a support group once a week. José's father didn't feel qualified to talk about these issues with his wife and so began to distance himself from her. She had many emotional highs and lows, and José could tell that she needed more support at home.

José could see from the outside what his father wasn't able to see. His father was reacting instinctively without recognizing the effect it was having on his marriage and on his other family relationships.

One Sunday afternoon, José invited his father to play a round a golf, and on the links he had a heart-to-heart talk with him. After hearing from his caring son, José's father knew that he needed to

> The longer we are silent, the longer we are hurting the next generation.

begin to move toward his wife again and be the nurturing, listening, loving husband she needed now more than ever. José's conversation with his father that day was one of the most important things he could have done for his family, for it opened up a line of communication that has remained open to this day.

To help break the generational curse, remember that in walking with your hurting parent toward the light at the end of the tunnel, you also need to take care of yourself. I think we often buy into the lie that we can never do too much for others, but that is so harmful. We need to spend time in relationships that allow us to take a deep breath and recharge. To be real with you, I struggle with overdoing it. I have to remind myself—and often my circle of inspiration will remind me— to slow down. I know I must be careful, and so should you.

Supporting someone who is going through the healing process from sexual abuse can be very draining. It will require courage and a substantial investment of time, emotional energy, and prayer. If you yourself were ever victimized, it can also trigger your own painful memories.

Don't feel guilty or selfish for taking care of yourself and your many emotions. It's normal to feel helpless, guilty, out of control, angry, frustrated, or overprotective. Find a safe place to talk about these emotions. Talk to a trusted friend or family member, or see a counselor yourself. Just as you are part of the circle surrounding your parent, you need to have your own circle surrounding you. It will be a breath of fresh air to you when you feel discouraged or overwhelmed.

If you have your own children, you must talk with them about sexual abuse. The longer we are silent, the longer we are hurting the next generation. When we don't communicate with those who are following us, we are allowing generational sin to continue its cycle.

Queen Silvia of Sweden said, "Sexual abuse is a global problem, and it's increasing. It's a taboo subject. It's a delicate question. But if you don't talk about it, then the children will continue suffering." Yet even in our sex-saturated culture, many parents are not only not talking to their children about sexual abuse; they're not even talking to them about sex.

Alisha's parents left it to others to talk to her about uncomfortable topics like sex and sexual abuse. However, Alisha's teachers, pastor, and doctor were leaving it to her parents to have those conversations. With no one taking responsibility, Alisha was completely unprepared when a friend of the family began molesting her. No one had ever talked to Alisha's parents about these important parts of life either, and they perpetuated this pattern to the detriment of their own children.

My mother and I have decided to not allow the effects of abuse to continue on in our family. By confronting the sexual abuse committed against us and seeking the Lord's healing in our relationships, we are saying no to this sin being passed on to my children and to future generations. Instead of hiding our heads in the sand, we are drawing a line in it.

A smooth sandy slate lies before all of us. We can choose to address the behaviors and problems that have replicated themselves in our family tree, or we can look the other way, hide our secrets, and allow more evil to creep into our family and our kids' lives. Survivors, let's gather up the courage to say no more! Let's boldly confront the sins of the fathers and decide that their sins will no longer be our family name.

This is not all up to me. I can't carry this load alone. It's too great for any one person. This desire to see a shift in the next generation has to begin with you. Your passion and concern is what can impact the lives of those closest to you. I'm not talking about being a high-profile mover and shaker. I'm talking about simply being someone who is willing to be a voice that says, "No more!"

We must not allow this secret to continue in our families, in our communities, or in our churches any longer. If we don't do anything about it now, it will continue to the next generation and to all the generations to come. But if we follow God's leading as Elijah did—even though it's through very difficult circumstances—He can make us a source of life to others. For the sake of the next generation, it's time to choose life.

THE REST of the Story

When we last saw the widow of Zarephath, she was on the brink of making a life-or-death decision. Which did she choose? She chose life, and as a result, her child lived. "So she did as Elijah said, and she and Elijah and her son continued to eat for many days. There was always enough flour and olive oil left in the containers, just as the Lord had promised through Elijah" (1 Kings 17:15–16).

But just when we think that the story has had a happy ending, Scripture surprises us. It tells us that the widow's son suddenly became ill and that he became worse and worse until he finally stopped breathing. Her son's life had been snuffed out, and so had her hope for the future, for without him, she would have no one to provide for her in her old age. Now she was totally helpless. She had no choices to make or actions to take. She had come to the end of herself.

In her anguish, the widow wondered if the prophet's presence in her house had attracted God's attention to her sin and drawn His anger. "Have you come here to point out my sins and kill my son?" she asked (v.18).

Elijah was as shocked by this turn of events as the widow was. But instead of trying to give her a glib answer, he took the child from his mother's arms, carried him up the stairs to the room where he was staying, laid the body on his bed, and asked God if He had killed the child. God's no must have reverberated in his soul, for the next thing Elijah did was to stretch himself over the boy's body three times and cry to God to return the boy to life. God answered

Elijah's prayer and breathed life back into the boy's lungs.

God wants to help us deal with the toxic effects of the evil acts of others so that we and our children can live. But if we aren't at the point where we've come to the end of ourselves, we're not at the point where we can do them any good. On his own, Elijah couldn't give the widow's son new life. God doesn't hold us responsible for something we don't have the power to do. Just as Elijah wasn't responsible for resuscitating the widow's son, you aren't responsible for healing your parent.

Although you can love, listen to, pray for, encourage, and walk beside a survivor on her journey, you can never heal her. That's God's responsibility, and He will carry this burden for you. Allow the Lord to work through you, as Elijah did. As you humbly place yourself at His disposal, God will breathe new life into her through you.

A Life Letter

Dear Adult Child . . .

If you're a child of a survivor of rape or sexual abuse, know that you aren't alone. There are many of us throughout this country and the world walking in your shoes. I recently discovered that my mother was a victim of rape, but rather than shunning this news like some might, I embraced it as an opportunity to help her heal. Now I'm here to encourage you to stand up and do the same because I know the difference it can make. The road has seemed long and dark at times, but as Nicole says, "There is light at the end of the tunnel." We just need to take the right steps to get there.

First, we must acknowledge that none of our parent's pain is our fault. Oftentimes their pain will cause them to lash out at us with harmful words or even abusive behavior, but we must understand that their actions aren't really directed at us. It's a fact of life that hurting people hurt others. Know that your parent's actions don't come from feelings about you, but from feelings that stem from abuse and haven't yet been dealt with.

Forgiveness is an important step if we want to be a source of encouragement and support for our hurting parents and help them see the light that we see. We need to forgive them for all the hurt and tears they've caused us because that's what enables us to embark on the healing journey with them. We can't genuinely encourage our parents if we can't forgive them for the hurt they have caused us.

When my mother shared with me that she was a rape survivor, all the pieces of my childhood fell into place. All of a sudden it made perfect sense why she had said and done such hurtful things to me while I growing up. Her disclosure shed light in the darkness and helped me release her from the chains that bound our relationship because I hadn't forgiven her. When we see our parent's own hurt, we begin to understand, and once we understand we can finally begin to forgive. We must always remember that just as we didn't ask to be a child of a victim, our parent didn't ask to be a victim. Holding on to bitterness and anger toward our parents will only cause them to feed off the same emotions. We must let go of all of our pain and move on so that they can do the same.

Just as we need encouragement, so do they. They need someone to take them by the hand and walk down the path of healing with them. Who better than us, their own kids? When our parents are feeling down, we must remind them of the hope that Jesus gives us and encourage them to hold on and push through.

At first, it might seem a little bit awkward to be encouraging your parent, but that's part of every healthy relationship, regardless of the age difference. As Paul wrote to Timothy, "Don't let anyone look down on you because you are young, but set an example for the believers in speech, in life, in love, in faith, and in purity" (1 Timothy 4:12 NIV).

We must follow Paul's advice with regard to our parents. We mustn't let anything make us afraid of opening up the lines of communication with them. We must voice our support and always offer them our listening ear. Don't let your parent go through this alone. Stick by her side and cheer her on the whole way. Always remind her that you're in this together to the very end. More often than not, you'll find that's just what she has been waiting to hear.

—Summer

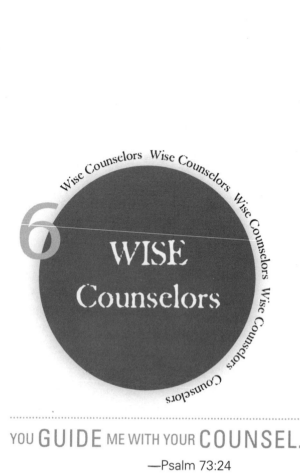

6

WISE
Counselors

Wise Counselors Wise Counselors Wise Counselors Wise Counselors Counselors

YOU **GUIDE** ME WITH YOUR **COUNSEL.**
—Psalm 73:24

My husband, Matt, is training to be an emergency-room physician. Many of the people who come to the emergency room as the result of some trauma are in need of resuscitation, so Matt has spent a long time observing and being observed by mentors who are helping him learn to literally breathe life back into people. The wise counsel of his experienced and knowledgeable mentors is molding Matt into the effective lifesaving physician he longs to be.

Mentors who are willing to teach us from their own life experiences and model for us what we desire to become can have a profound impact on all of us. Such people are found in all walks of life. They can be professional counselors, parents, pastors, coaches, coworkers, or friends. They can be any of the people in our circle of inspiration who, because of their life experiences, their training, or both, can give us wise counsel that breathes new life into us as they walk alongside us on our healing journey.

To me, true mentors are people who see our potential and have a desire to invest in our life by speaking wisdom and truth to our circumstances and by modeling what we aspire to be. Mentors recognize our longing to heal and mature, and they guide us toward better choices and healthier relationships. They know what the path ahead looks like for, in one way or another, they have traveled it themselves. Because they know the pitfalls along the way, their wise counsel helps keep us on track on our healing journey.

SOMEONE WHO NEEDED
Wise Counselors

Job was a righteous man, and God had blessed him in an incredible way. He had seven sons and three daughters, and he was the richest man in the land of Uz. But then disaster struck. In a single day he lost all of his children and all of his wealth. And that was only the beginning. Soon he lost his health, and he was in so much pain that he wanted to die, which was exactly what his wife advised him to do (Job:1–2).

Then three of Job's friends came to comfort him. At first, they seemed to respond to Job's plight with genuine sympathy. Mourning right along with Job, they wept, tore their clothes, and covered themselves with ashes. For a week they just sat with him, not saying a word. But when they finally spoke, their words only made Job's suffering worse.

With dogmatic certainty instead of wisdom, Job's friends set out to convince him that his suffering was the result of some sin in his life. Since they knew that God rewards what is right, they reasoned that doing what is right always brings peace and prosperity, while doing what is wrong is always the reason for suffering. Since Job was suffering, they concluded that he was a sinner. And they told him so—over and over and over. Instead of supporting Job, his counselors ended up condemning him.

CAN YOU RELATE?

A survivor of childhood sexual abuse, Maddie was also raped in college. Never having felt safe enough or courageous enough to share her story about her childhood abuse, she had turned to the path of addiction to alcohol to cope with her pain. But after she was date-raped, she felt that she had reached the end of her rope, and she decided to seek a listening ear. She needed help. She needed a word of comfort. She needed a wise counselor. So she went to the pastor of a local church.

As Maddie's story began to unfold, the pastor responded in

much the same way that Job's friends did. When she told him about the date rape, he asked questions that made her feel as if it had been her own fault because she had been drinking. He told her that in order to be welcome in the church she would have to repent of her sins and immediately change her lifestyle.

Maddie's counselor probably thought he was guiding her onto the right path, but his critical attitude only pushed her farther away from it. Feeling worse about herself than ever, she returned to her isolation and continued to rely upon alcohol to cope with her pain.

WHY MENTORING
Relationships Sometimes Fail

As Maddie's story shows, some of us run from a mentoring relationship because we feel misjudged and condemned by the one attempting to counsel us. Others of us were victimized by someone who took advantage of our trust and loyalty while filling the role of mentor in our life. These are two reasons it can seem risky to allow someone who assumes this role into our circle.

Although being misjudged or betrayed is very painful, it doesn't mean that we'll never have a successful mentoring relationship. There are wise counselors out there. That said, there's no need to rush into a mentoring relationship. In a get-rich-quick, fast-food, diet-pill society, we tend to expect instant results. But survivors who are open to and ready for a mentor will find that time and patience are often key to having a successful mentoring relationship. We have to know the person we're dealing with, and that takes time.

Liz says that the person who has been most influential in her healing process is her mentor, Dee, who is on staff at her Christian college. But Dee didn't just pick Liz randomly and ask her if she could mentor her and help her heal from sexual abuse. If she had, it probably would have freaked Liz out! "Dee was always around when I went to chapel or had a class in her building," Liz says. "She was very welcoming whenever I saw her, which made me want to get to know her. I knew that I needed someone older and much wiser to talk to, and Dee's warm personality drew me to her."

Dee reminds me of the many other amazing mentors I've run into on college campuses in the years I've been speaking to students. Being a person who is available, welcoming, nonjudgmental, gentle, and authentic stands out like a familiar face in a crowd of strangers. And sexual abuse survivors like Liz and me are drawn to them.

"I had been praying that God would bring a mentor into my life, and over the summer I found the courage to send Dee an e-mail," Liz says. "As we began communicating, I started to trust her, and eventually I opened up about my past. When I came back to school in the fall, she told me that she wanted to be the first person I saw. That helped me see that she really cared about me. She shared with me about her own abuse, which made me feel safe enough to share more about my experience. That's when we started meeting regularly and sorting through a lot of my issues.

"Dee was not one of those who say, 'I'll always be there for you,' but then slowly drift away. She was very intentional about having a relationship with me. Once I knew that she wasn't going to give up on me, I knew I could trust her. She always tells me that she is never going to stop loving me, caring about me, or being there for me. For once in my life, after being so hurt and misled through love and trust in my childhood, I could actually allow myself to believe it."

Liz says that Dee's belief in her was what gave her hope for the future. "Not only did she believe in me, but she helped me to begin to believe in myself. She never let me say 'I'm giving up' even though that's what I felt like doing. She made me see that there's a light at the end of this and that my life will be richer because I allowed myself to face the truth. I hope that someday I can help someone as much as Dee has helped me."

Significant moments of growth and healing occurred in my own life during seasons in which I was being mentored. Like Liz, I recognize the important role that mentoring has played in bringing me to where I am today. As a result of the impact that various mentors have made on my own life, I have a burning desire to return the favor by investing myself in the lives around me. I long to make the same level of difference in someone else's life and future. This explains why so many mentors do what they do. They long to give from what they have received.

The mentoring relationship can be a very positive experience for any survivor when it's based on realistic expectations. Establishing them in the beginning lays the foundation for a healthy, lasting relationship by creating trust, allowing healing to flow through the mentoring process, and strengthening a survivor's circle of inspiration. However, a mentoring relationship can fail if a survivor has unrealistic expectations of it. Ultimately, the survivor will feel let down and may withdraw from the relationship altogether.

Survivors who feel great trust in their mentors can be tempted to look to them for the solution to every problem and the final answer for every question they have. Such expectations can create an unhealthy attachment that will not only destroy the mentoring relationship, but also cause great pain to both the survivor and mentor. No one can meet all our deepest needs, and no one can give us all the answers. Only God can do those things. Looking for this in people will bring disappointment, failure, and resentment, because even the best mentor in the world is human and thus far from perfect.

Lydia loved and trusted her mentor, Gigi, more than anyone else in her circle. So whenever she was going through a difficult situation—whether she was feeling lonely, having a bad day, or just wanting to talk to someone—she called Gigi. When she wasn't calling Gigi, she was e-mailing her. When she wasn't e-mailing her, she was text messaging her. But if Gigi wasn't available or didn't respond immediately, Lydia felt neglected, unimportant, and angry. Soon she emotionally distanced herself from Gigi and began to lash out at her and say cruel things to her.

For her part, Gigi had no idea why Lydia was treating her this way. All she knew was that she felt bombarded. She loved Lydia, but she couldn't possibly be there for her every moment. She was busy with her own life and duties and couldn't respond to Lydia's every beck and call. She assumed that Lydia understood this, but Lydia didn't understand because the two had never discussed their expectations of the relationship. Not understanding where to draw the line, Lydia pulled out of a mentoring relationship that could have provided her with a great deal of guidance and support on her healing journey.

Living in isolation and anonymity can also prevent a survivor from having a positive mentoring relationship. Mentors can't know that you're longing to be mentored if they don't know what you're going through or that you even exist. Those around us don't always recognize our needs unless we tell them. So be willing to take the first step. Pray about it, asking the Lord to bring you just the right person, the very one He has chosen to fill this role within your circle. As the Lord directs you, seek out a trustworthy mentor and slowly invite him into your circle of inspiration.

We need people like this in our circle for far too often those who try to show us the way are like Job's friends, who although they wanted to help and thought that they were supporting him, instead were tearing him down.

MENTORING A SURVIVOR

Becoming a mentor begins with establishing trust. When we were betrayed as children, we learned that adults couldn't be trusted. Many of us couldn't even trust members of our own family. Now as adults, we tend to believe the lie that no one can be trusted. As a result, our relationships are often unhealthy.

Because of her abuse, trust was really difficult for Loren. She had a great fear of rejection and was afraid of what Karen would think of her if she knew the truth. Loren had to learn to trust again, even though everything in her was screaming at her to run away, just as she had done in the past. Loren and Karen had to work through those issues together. Karen had to keep proving herself and not give up when Loren revealed her insecurity; Loren had to push herself to be vulnerable again and accept that God created us to need each other and to help each other.

The most important thing that Karen did to establish trust was simply to believe Loren. "The fact that Karen believed me without hesitation was huge in building my trust," Loren says. Karen was also a wise mentor in the way she used her ears, her eyes, and her voice.

Karen was willing to spend time just listening. No matter how many times Loren needed to talk through her anger, her feeling of being at fault, or the issue of forgiveness, Karen listened patiently and intently. Mentors, like everyone else in a survivor's circle of inspiration, must use their ears to listen to the story of a survivor's life. We listen for clues to what kind of life she longs to have and what kind of ministry she longs to be a part of. We listen for God's voice speaking His truth. And we also listen for the lies and false beliefs that are keeping her from becoming all she was created to be.

MENTORS HELP survivors discover their true identity, passion, and calling.

While Karen listened carefully, she also looked closely. I believe that the Lord often reveals to the eyes of a mentor a treasure that no one else has yet seen. God helps mentors committed to doing His work see in others what He Himself sees, and He uses them to help uncover that hidden treasure. Mentors have the ability to look beyond the brokenness, the wounds, and the hurt to catch a glimpse of the beauty beneath the protective layers. As mentors, our main role is to be a mirror to survivors, asking questions to provoke self-reflection and to uncover the things in them that are holding them back from being all they were created to be. Mentors help survivors discover their true identity, passion, and calling.

When Karen spoke, she chose her words with care. She didn't give Loren pat spiritual answers simply because that's what she was used to doing or because she didn't know what else to say. She resisted the urge to respond in "Christianese," especially in the beginning when Loren was clearly not interested in that language. And when it was time, Karen shared truths about God through His Word by using analogies that helped Loren replace lies with truth. Karen also wasn't afraid of silence because she knew that sometimes all Loren needed was someone to be with her.

One of the most important traits of wise mentors is that when they speak, they use their voice to speak the truth about God, not to condemn. That's where Job's counselors and Maddie's mentor made their big mistake. A mentor's goal is to keep survivors in a circle of inspiration so they can breathe in new life and begin to heal. But judgmental comments only pile more undeserved shame upon them, make them retreat from the circle, and push them farther away from God and healing.

"When I finally decided to take a risk and tell Karen everything," Loren says, "she responded with a love and compassion that I never thought I would receive. She didn't judge me. She wasn't afraid to talk about the abuse, but she never made me feel uncomfortable. She simply asked questions in order to understand where I was coming from and help me verbalize what I was thinking. When she spoke, it was to lovingly offer me advice based on biblical truths. Because of the way she has mentored me, for the first time in my life I feel I don't have to hide or pretend all of the time."

As mentors, you can be genuine about your feelings without appearing to condemn or blame the other person. I have found that using the word *I* helps a lot when I'm talking about my feelings. Instead of saying, "You confused me," I say, "I'm confused by what you just said. Can you explain?" Instead of saying, "You made me angry," I say, "I feel angry." Instead of saying, "You're telling me too much," I say, "It's hard for me to hear all at once all the painful things you've been through. If it's okay with you, can we pray together now and then plan a time to talk again?"

Another way to avoid saying anything that sounds judgmental is to not ask questions like "Why did you go there with him?" or "Why didn't you leave?" or "Why didn't you tell someone right away?" Questions like these tend to be condemning, for they make a survivor think that you are blaming her for what happened.

When Trish finally found the courage to tell her mentor, Cathy, that she had been raped in the bathroom of a college dorm where she was attending a party, Cathy asked her why she had gone to the party in the first place. Her words told Trish that she had put herself in a situation to be raped and deserved the consequences. Feeling condemned, Trish shut down.

Danny, a youth counselor, was trying to help sixteen-year-old

Bianca come to terms with why she was raped. As part of the discussion, he called attention to her choice of clothing as something to consider. Coming from someone she considered a mentor and one of the only voices of truth in her life, Danny's words reinforced the lie that Bianca had deserved to be raped. Though Danny's motives were pure, these blaming words sucked out of Bianca the little breath she had.

Once trust has been established, a mentor should seek to hold a survivor accountable, but only in context of compassionate understanding and encouragement. We can cause a survivor a world of hurt if we come across as judgmental, even though we may just be trying to help him make better choices. Even if you have some doubts about the validity of the details of the incident, act as if you believe her. Don't promise her that you won't tell someone else, as there might come a time that you'll have to talk to the authorities. But by all means, don't gossip. Poorly chosen words, words spoken at the wrong time, and gossip can destroy all the trust it has taken months to build.

When I speak to a survivor, I use my voice to tell my story, to express my belief in the person I am investing myself in, and to fuel any hope or passion she might have. I use it to speak truth to whatever lies and false beliefs she believes. I use it to encourage her to dream big and to pursue her dreams with confidence. And I use my voice to help reveal the hand of God as I see it working in her life.

Mentoring is not a hierarchical or one-sided relationship. Mentors are learners as well as teachers. "Karen kept reminding me that our friendship was mutual and that she was learning just as much from me as she was helping me," Loren said. Though a mentor will have more experience than the survivor in critical areas, mentoring is a give-and-take relationship in which both people are teaching and both are learning. Understanding this helps build the trust that is vital to an effective mentoring relationship. If you're learning from a survivor in a mentoring relationship, make sure she knows it. This helps keep the relationship on the right path.

To be a wise mentor, our motives must be pure. Mentoring isn't about us. It's about others. Mentors must be unselfish and humble, never seeking status or affirmation, but only for ways to serve. The moment we begin to think highly of ourselves or try to meet our own needs by mentoring someone is the moment when the mentoring relationship takes a turn for the worse. We take both the survivor and ourselves off the road of life onto a detour that ends in disappointment and pain. Don't allow impure motives to destroy a potentially life-changing, healing relationship with a survivor.

Loren says that another thing that caused her to trust Karen was "the fact that she was honest about her life and real in her relationship with God." Wise mentors strive to be what they want to see a survivor become. At their best, they are imitators of Christ who attract others by the way they live and then invite them to follow along as they seek to be the same. In essence, the life of a mentor should say, "Come along and follow my lead, as I use the things I've learned to better follow Jesus."

We can't require something of others that we're not willing to strive for ourselves. In helping another survivor look at her heart, her character, her brokenness, I have had to look at my own. Being a mentor puts us in a position where we are looked to as an example; therefore we must take into account our own words, actions, lifestyle, and heart. Mentoring should make us hold ourselves accountable and push us to make sure that we are walking the talk.

Wise counselors are patient. A friend of Aimee's really listened the first time she told her secret and at first was very supportive. Since then, however, she seems to get annoyed whenever Aimee brings it up. "It's not like I bring it up a lot," Aimee says. "It's just when I get back from counseling or have a bad dream at night. I will sometimes want to share with her and she kind of shuts me down as if this should be resolved or something. Perhaps it's true, but I need her to understand where I am right now and that I really am working on it."

There are no shortcuts on the road to healing. Reassure the person you are mentoring that you'll stick with her and do everything you can to help her. And in the days and weeks and months ahead, prove to her that all of this is true.

Shannon's roommate in college was the residence hall assistant.

She was a wise mentor who helped Shannon by sticking with her and taking appropriate steps to help her along the way. "She learned early on how to recognize when I was having bad memory dreams and to wake me up," Shannon told me. "That couldn't have been easy for her because I often woke up swinging at whatever touched me. She also went through all my stuff one day and confiscated every sharp object she thought I could possibly use to hurt myself. If I needed it for real she would get it for me, but otherwise it stayed hidden. I still have no idea where she hid all that stuff!"

Karen reassured Loren that she was in this for the long haul and that she wasn't going anywhere. She encouraged Loren to tell God how she felt, explaining that He could handle it and that she shouldn't be afraid to share openly with Him. Initially, praying was difficult for Loren, so Karen prayed with her and for her. Loren said, "I know she went to God on my behalf many, many times. For a long time, she was God's hands and feet to me." Mentoring is partnering with the Holy Spirit, who alone knows how to reach a survivor in a way that will bring healing.

To go the distance, both the mentor and the survivor have to live balanced lives. "We both made sure the friendship was balanced," Loren says. "On some of the tough days, Karen discerned that maybe it was just time to laugh and have fun. That was part of my healing too!" Make sure you balance your relationship with other activities and other people.

Don't give up when you feel like a broken record or are tired of reassuring her or having to keep proving yourself. She doesn't mean to be annoying. She's just learning to trust again. Remember that repetition fosters learning and that you're helping her even when you might feel as if you aren't.

When I think about the role of a mentor in the healing journey of a sexual abuse survivor, I think about my high school track coach, Mr. Wendt. He was a runner himself, so he knew the ins and outs of the sport, the track, and what it took to win. When I was running a 400-meter race, Coach Wendt would run from one side of the track to the other to cheer me on. When I reached the 100-meter mark, he would be there, yelling and ringing a loud cowbell.

As soon as I sprinted past him, he would run across the football field to the other side of the track and wait for me at the 300-meter mark before the final straightaway. Cheering, clapping, and calling my name, he helped give me that extra push past my opponents and over the finish line.

Mr. Wendt's role in my high school track career is a picture of the role I hope every mentor will play in the healing journey of an abuse survivor. A mentor should be running up ahead to cheer her on. He should call out her name as she sprints toward the light at the end of the tunnel of healing. Like Mr. Wendt, he should be the ultimate encourager.

THE REST of the Story

From the very beginning of Job's story we know what he and his counselors don't: Job's suffering has nothing to do with anything he has or hasn't done. His suffering was the result of circumstances he knew nothing about, wasn't responsible for, and couldn't control.

Just as the Pharisees were trying to get at Jesus through the woman caught in adultery, Satan was trying to get at God through the righteous Job. To bring down God, Satan attacked Job's relationship with Him, and the instruments he used were Job's well-meaning but misguided friends. Their big mistake was trying to give Job answers that only God can give. Only He knows why someone is suffering, and only He knows the part that person's suffering plays in His purpose and plan.

In the first few chapters of Job, we learn what to say—and what not to say—when people who are suffering need an encouraging word. To give Job's friends their due, it cost them something to show that they cared. They traveled a long way to express their grief, sat silently with him for an entire week, and listened when he spoke. Yet in failing to acknowledge that God has many reasons for allowing the innocent to suffer, Job's counselors ended up being "miserable comforters" who condemned him instead of giving him hope for the future.

Genuine mentors can make a world of difference to survivors who need someone to give them wise counsel and inspire them with hope. One of the greatest gifts a mentor can give is to create and maintain a positive, honest, and affirming relationship with someone who has never experienced anything of that kind. Add to all of this your time, true compassion, and unconditional acceptance—which all speak louder than most words ever will—and you will make a huge impact on a survivor who is trying to sort out her relationships and find hope for the future.

A Life Letter

Dear Mentor . . .

The word *mentor* originated in Greek mythology. Mentor was the friend to whom Odysseus, when departing for Troy, gave the charge of his household. The word means a wise and trusted counselor. If you are considering or already have been mentoring a survivor, recognize that this is the role she is giving you. She is putting you in charge of her "household" of pain.

I'd like to share with you the most important things I've learned about mentoring in more than thirty years as a counselor for both victims and offenders in cases of childhood sexual abuse.

First, know that no matter how much genuine compassion you have, it is finite. It's only through your own ongoing relationship with Jesus that you can be a conduit of healing for another. Let your mentoree see that without your faith in God, your close personal relationship with Jesus, and your listening to the Holy Spirit, you would never be able to minister to her.

I'd also caution you not to quote Scripture as a quick response to deep pain. While God's Word is absolutely true, when and how you use it can make all the difference in the world. This is going to be especially true for those survivors who considered their offenders believers.

Also, don't rush forgiveness. We don't expect someone with a broken leg to run a marathon. A survivor who has yet to get in touch with his pain still has a broken leg. Don't try to make him run a marathon just yet. Forgiveness will come. Survivors can understand the enormity of what they are forgiving only after they have realized the full extent of their losses. Unaccompanied by such understanding, their forgiveness will be false and can lead to deeper problems later on.

Accept and listen to their anger at God or the church. It is a rare survivor who doesn't experience such anger. Part of the process of healing is bringing all the pain out of the darkness and into the light so that it can be healed. Be sensitive to the season your mentoree is in on his journey. Simply put, don't talk to him about Jesus unless you are being Jesus to him.

Don't judge. Generally most survivors are too hard on themselves and don't need anyone else to point out their mistakes. A good mentor will love them enough to love them right where they are—and then love them enough to not let them stay there.

Most likely, there will be times you'll need to confront your mentoree about her thinking or behavior in order for her to move on. However, discernment and timing are crucial. I have a saying that has served me well over the years: "You must build a bridge before you drive a tank over it." The best mentors I know have learned the art of building bridges and steering tanks! Just make sure your bridges are constructed of trust and respect and that your relationship is solid before you lovingly confront a survivor.

Finally, always be a light in the darkness. Sometimes your flame will be more like a candle than a torch. Sometimes it will resemble a glowing ember. Regardless, it is a light, and as long as the source of your light is the flame of Jesus' love, He will use it to offer your mentoree hope and healing. May God use you to help bring broken survivors out of their darkness and "breathe" once again.

—Victoria

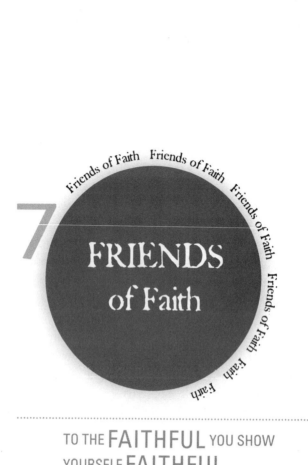

7

FRIENDS
of Faith

Friends of Faith Friends of Faith Friends of Faith Friends of Faith Faith Faith

TO THE FAITHFUL YOU SHOW
YOURSELF FAITHFUL.

—Psalm 18:25

Mahatma Gandhi once said, "You must be the change you wish to see in the world." I love that. I think that is the essence of my own mission during my time here on earth—to be the change I long to see happen.

My ministry is built upon the fact that I am one person God has ignited with a flame of passion to make a difference in the lives of broken people, specifically survivors of childhood sexual abuse. I take that flame with me to audiences all over the world. Sometimes I get to witness an entire college campus breathing so much air on the flame that it lights up like a forest fire, spreading to thousands of others.

I pray for the same thing to happen in churches, for a church is meant to be the purest example of a circle of inspiration that we can find on earth. Unfortunately, many churches are so protected, so guarded, so silent that their people seem to be incombustible. Too many churches bring hurting people in only to have them leave with more wounds than they arrived with.

Where will these broken people go if friends of faith don't bring them to Jesus, welcome them in the church, love them, and inspire them with the hope of a better life? Faithful followers of Jesus will reach out to survivors in compassion, just as Jesus would.

SOMEONE WHO NEEDED
Friends of Faith

After His first preaching tour in Galilee, Jesus returned to His home base in Capernaum. When the news spread that He was back home, everyone rushed to the house where He was staying. Soon it was so packed that there wasn't room for any more people, even outside the door.

Mark 2:3–4 says that while Jesus was preaching God's Word to the people gathered there, four men arrived carrying a paralyzed man on a mat. They couldn't bring their friend to Jesus through the door because of the crowd, so they ripped a hole in the roof above His head and lowered the mat until the man was right in front of Jesus.

I find these men's love for their suffering friend so inspiring! The man's affliction made it impossible for him to get to Jesus by himself. He needed four friends of faith to carry him. His friends believed that Jesus could heal him, and they were determined to take him to where He was. They had to be creative and assertive and persistent, but they got him there. In the same way, true friends of faith can help bring survivors to Jesus for healing.

CAN YOU RELATE?

Paula was someone who knew that she needed friends of faith to help her heal. But unlike the paralytic, she didn't have those kinds of friends. Nor did she find them where she most expected to.

As a survivor of childhood sexual abuse, for years Paula isolated herself from relationships because she was afraid of being hurt again. Finally, she reached a place of complete emptiness. She remembered having heard as a child that Jesus loved her, no matter what she had done or experienced, and she knew that His followers were called to do the same. In the hope of finding that kind of love and care, one Sunday she walked through the doors of the church located just around the corner from her apartment building.

She slid into the back row, worrying about what everyone thought of her. However, she was greeted with smiles, hellos, and handshakes, and that was enough to bring her back. As the weeks passed, she began to feel more comfortable letting people in the church get to know her little by little. She took a giant step down her healing path when she started going to a women's Bible study group.

The women in her group sensed that there was something bothering Paula, but they never asked—except Kate. Kate let Paula know that she was available if Paula ever needed a listening ear. Paula, craving the kind of relationship that she had pushed away for so long, got real and shared her story with Kate. How freeing it was for Paula to let the secret out! Even better, Kate responded with heartfelt sadness for the trauma Paula had endured throughout her childhood. Paula thanked Kate for being willing to listen and asked her to keep her story confidential.

Later that week, Paula arrived late to the Bible study. As she walked down the hallway toward the great room, she heard the women sharing their weekly prayer requests. She came to an abrupt halt when she heard Kate's voice. She was telling Paula's most intimate secret to the entire group in the form of a prayer request.

Feeling betrayed, Paula turned around and walked out the door. Instead of finding life-giving air in a circle of inspiration, she felt more suffocated than ever.

WHY WE OFTEN FIND IT HARD
to Breathe in Church

When I was a teenager, I realized that through prayer I could always enter the presence of God to work through my feelings and find comfort. But at the same time, I wanted Him to be sitting there with me in the flesh. I told Him in my prayer journal that our time together was really great, but that if He could somehow put some skin on, it would be even better. I wanted someone to be there with me, to hold me, to speak audibly to me, and to invest some of his or her precious time in my life. I think that's the prayer of many of us. And I think that God calls other believers to be the answer to our prayer.

Sadly, I hear from many other survivors who believe that their church isn't willing or able to be part of their circle of inspiration. Some, in fact, believe that their church's attitudes and agendas have cut off the life-giving air that they so desperately need.

Let's be honest. Not every church is a healthy church. Many

today aren't functioning according to God's standards. They are insensitive to the needs of their own members, not to mention those in the broader community, and they are sticking their heads in the sand or telling victims to hush. Worse, they are covering up sexual sin.

When I speak in churches or at Christian schools, I often run into people who tell me that sexual abuse has never been and never will be a problem there. Sadly, this is the exact opposite of what I have found.

Ashley's abuser was her father, the pastor of a large church in her community. Every time she reached out for help from people in the church family, they responded with things like, "Well, you're probably the only one he did this to, and he is the pastor, so just let it go." As a young boy, Chad was the victim of the popular, long-established pastor of his family's church. Today as an adult, he understandably struggles to trust others or to allow true friends of faith to come alongside him on his healing journey.

When churches try to cover up sexual sin to protect their reputation or sources of financial support in the community, they not only allow abuse to continue, but also create fertile ground for per petrators to plant themselves.

A wealthy, well-respected man in Sandi's church sexually abused her when she was young. When Sandi told her mother about the things he had done to her in the bathroom during Sunday school, her mother told the senior pastor of the church. To her surprise, he asked her to keep quiet, as this "rumor" could ruin the church. He also told her that if it got out, her family would be removed from their church body. Sandi's mother kept on seeking justice, but the church leadership kept on covering up this man's crime. He continued to serve in the church and to have access to other potential victims.

Covering up sexual sin drives survivors from the church, and refraining from evil deeds isn't enough to bring them back. Paul tells followers of Christ to "take no part in the worthless deeds of evil and darkness; instead, expose them" (Ephesians 5:11). We who are called to live in the light must take this call seriously with regard to sexual abuse. Silence suggests approval, protects the sin, and allows this evil to continue to tear apart relationships—and churches.

Perpetuating abuse and covering it up are not the only things that can keep survivors from forming healing relationships in the church. As was the case with Paula, well-meaning friends of faith can drive away a survivor by not keeping what she tells them confidential. Like Kate, a trusted recipient of "the secret" often says to someone else in the church, "What I am about to tell you is top secret! You can't tell anyone. I'm only telling you this so you can pray for her."

This is like that game of "telephone operator" we played when we were kids. Before you know it, not only is half the church talking about it, but the story has also totally changed. And in the end, the survivor who has finally found the courage to tell feels betrayed by the very people she should have been able to trust.

Another way the church can push survivors away is by introducing the issue of forgiveness at the wrong time or in the wrong way. I have personally experienced the unmatched freedom found in forgiveness, but I have also experienced the hurt that has come from the demands some Christians placed on me regarding it. Advice like "You just need to forgive" doesn't help. In fact, it's harmful. Being told to forgive at the onset of healing can increase feelings of guilt and shame to insupportable levels.

When a survivor has just opened up and is beginning to accept the reality of what has happened to him, he's usually struggling with blaming himself for the abuse. What he needs is a season to be angry and place the blame where it belongs. Forgiveness will come further down the road. Insisting that someone forgive his abuser can hinder the healing process by making it more difficult for him to accept the truth about his abuse, himself, and God's great love and concern for him right where he is.

Jenny, who recently opened up to a friend at church, said, "She was wonderful to me! I admitted to her that I had a lot of trouble forgiving my grandfather. She pointed out to me that what I needed to do first was to not take on guilt that wasn't my own. She said that forgiving my grandfather for his crime would come as I continued to heal. Hearing this from a Christian made all the difference."

Insisting that a survivor always focus on the positive doesn't help either. Some people think it's a Christian's duty to be happy at all times. But Ecclesiastes 3:4 says that there is a time to weep as well as a time to laugh. And Romans 12:15 says to "be happy with those who are happy, and weep with those who weep." This is what survivors need most—someone to walk beside them on the journey and to support them in all the ups and downs. This means not expecting a survivor to "put on a happy face."

It hurts me when I hear people in the church telling survivors to wear a mask and pretend, when what they really need to do is to get real. It may make life easier for the church for survivors to act as if life is always peachy, but we aren't called to minister to those who have no problems and thus no need to come to Jesus. "It is not the healthy who need a doctor, but the sick," Jesus said (Matthew 9:12 NIV). How can we know who needs healing if we tell broken people to smile and pretend that everything is fine?

We need to toss the myth of the perpetually happy Christian out the door. In this life, we are going to suffer. And it isn't all going to come from Satan. God is sometimes behind it for reasons He alone knows. I don't believe that He causes suffering, but I am certain that He allows it for His own purposes. Though I have suffered through the effects of abuse, God has used my suffering to make me better.

One of the greatest things that suffering has done for me is to help me understand just a bit of what Jesus went through for me. While He was on earth, Jesus' biggest concern was always with people's relationship with God. His greatest desire was that none of us live in darkness and despair, exiled from God's light and love. That's why He suffered the shame and the pain of the cross. When He became sin for us, God withdrew, and for the first time in all of eternity, Christ experienced being absolutely alone. Yet He willingly did this so that all of us could have a personal relationship with Him. Knowing this keeps my eyes focused on Him, for without Him I have no hope.

As survivors on the healing journey, we often wish that the path toward the light ahead had lampposts lining both sides and that there were no bumps or forks in the road. But that's never how it is. The truth is that we will always encounter dark places, obstacles in our way, and unexpected detours. God has designed our journey this way to make us stronger by teaching us to seek Him and rely on Him more. He uses our challenging and oftentimes painful circumstances to teach us that He works all things together for good and that we need to trust Him in that. He uses them to develop our character for what is to come—for all the relationships and experiences we don't even know about yet.

HIS GREATEST desire was that none of us live in darkness and despair, exiled from God's light and love.

When I look at my relationships today, I can see how God has allowed me to experience some painful things so that I could better understand and speak an encouraging word to other survivors. I know that part of His purpose in allowing me to suffer has been to mold me into the person He wants me to be and to better equip me for the ministry to which He has called me. Though it's often hard, I try to look not at the pain, but to the purpose behind the pain. That helps me through. Anyone who assumes that no true follower of Jesus should ever suffer is minimizing what God has planned for her life.

Don't get me wrong. I still don't have all the answers as to why certain bad things happen in my life or in yours. But I do know one thing: when we hurt, God hurts with us. In my loneliness, my grieving, my anger, or my hurt, I'm never alone. His Word assures me that He is with me through it all and that He cares. Peter says to "give all your worries and cares to God, for he cares about you" (1 Peter 5:7).

Our Lord is in touch with our feelings because at one time or another while He was on earth, He experienced every single one of them. He felt alone, angry, confused, abused, ignored, forsaken, abandoned, worthless, scorned, mocked, insulted, rejected, despised, used, taken advantage of, hurt, looked down upon, humiliated, trapped, weak, tired, speechless, overwhelmed with pain, pierced, victimized. When the Lord hears our cries, He understands, and He wants to heal us. And even though the church sometimes puts obstacles in our path, as followers of Christ, we are commanded to bring survivors to Him for healing.

BRINGING SURVIVORS TO
Jesus for Healing

When you become a follower of Christ, you join the family of God. We sometimes call this the "body of Christ." It refers to people all over the world who are united by their choice to love and follow Jesus. God tells us that it's important to meet together as a family regularly because we need one another to grow and be encouraged. Hebrews 10:25 says, "Let us not neglect our meeting together, as some people do, but encourage one another." So much encouragement can come from fellowship with others in a healthy community of faith.

I have found that small groups are the best way to provide for the needs of survivors in the church. The church Matt and I attend is very large, and our pastors could never meet every need that comes through the door each weekend. Meeting in small groups allows each of us to be Christ's heart, hands, eyes, and ears to those who are suffering from the effects of childhood sexual abuse or any other hurt in life.

Participating in a small group within the church was what helped Sophie overcome her tendency to form unhealthy attachments. She admits that she easily gets attached to her Christian friends. She places them on a pedestal in her mind and thinks they can do no wrong. As a result, she expects their every word and action to be perfect and the answer to her every need. But when they don't have time for her, when they respond to her with ignorance or insensitivity, or when they don't seem to care, Sophie is inevitably let down. Her Christian friends' failure to meet her unrealistic expectations reinforces the lie that no one really cares and that no one will ever understand.

Sophie got the help she needed when she found the courage to attend a recovery group for sexual abuse survivors at her church. She was scared to death when she went to the first meeting, but it was worth it in the end. In this circle she discovered that she wasn't alone, made new friendships with people struggling with similar issues, and received guidance and insight from a licensed counselor. Most important, Sophie learned that her friends' responses aren't going to be those of a trained counselor, pastor, or mentor. When she realized this, her expectations became realistic and her friendships grew stronger. Attending that recovery group was the beginning of much healing and freedom in Sophie's life.

As a circle of inspiration, the church should be a safe place where people can begin to truly know one another, where people can speak the truth in love out of a commitment to one another's greatest well-being. As a result of being abused as a child, Abby also had a problem with unhealthy attachments. When she finally decided to work on having healthy friendships, she began by honestly analyzing her past friendships to discover what had gone wrong. When she realized that she was too clingy, she told her small group at church about her problem and asked them to help her change this self-defeating behavior.

Once trust was established, Abby's friends of faith immediately began to support her by speaking the truth in love. They would ask her questions and pray for her. If they saw that she was beginning to cling to someone, they were honest with her about it.

"It's hard when the friend you are attached to tells you that you need to back off a little," Abby said. "But hearing it from friends at church who wanted to see me get healthy was much easier." Their support helped her stop the unhealthy behavior that was destroying her friendships. In the end, she found that she felt happier and freer by having a variety of friends instead of just one extremely close one.

Survivors aren't what some people assume: just a bunch of needy people with lots of problems. The very fact that we've survived means that we have even greater strength and gifting than we ourselves tend to believe. Our life experiences often give us a greater depth of understanding and compassion for others, as well as greater faith in the midst of some of the most unimaginable circumstances. Therefore, we have a great deal to bring to the church.

Having duties and responsibilities within the church helps make our life purpose driven. It demolishes the lie that we believe about ourselves: that we can't be trusted and can't contribute. Just helping with custodial needs or planning special events can be very healing to a sexual abuse survivor who feels inadequate, unaccepted, and like a misfit.

Marge is an adult survivor of childhood sexual abuse who works with her church's ministry to single moms. Having been a single mother herself, Marge knows that these women need to spend uninterrupted time with other single moms. So every month she helps plan a special dinner for them and arranges for child care during the meal. Not only is Marge touching the hearts and lives of single mothers with the love of Jesus and the church, but having the opportunity to use her gifts in this way has also heightened her self-confidence and self-esteem. Like many others survivors who have found a place to serve, Marge is blessed to be a blessing.

Education is key to preventing and breaking the cycle of violence among us. Speak up about these issues in your church. Help make your church a safer place for children. Examine the daily operations, the layout of the building, and children's ministry rooms. Do background checks on staff. Review your church's policies and procedures with regard to child abuse. Provide training workshops, put a licensed counselor on the staff, and support local Christian counseling services. Get connected with local resources. Know your limitations and network with other churches and community service organizations in order to provide well-rounded support to the individuals who come to you for help.

As the part of the body of Christ, believers are called to be His hands and reach out to fill the needs of those who are suffering. "When God's people are in need," Paul says, "be ready to help them. Always be eager to practice hospitality" (Romans 12:13).

After I broke my silence about my abuse, one family of faith in particular became a living example of Paul's command to show hospitality. They allowed my mother and me to stay in their home. They hid us and did all they could to make us feel safe. After my stepfather killed himself, they insisted that we continue to stay with them as long as we needed. They even cleaned up the mess left by my stepfather's suicide, which allowed us to move back into our home with less trauma. This is a picture of true hospitality and servanthood. That family was an amazing blessing to us in the time of our greatest need.

Churches and busy Christians, I pray you will be willing to look beyond the large crowds and busy schedules that stand in the way in order to see those in need and that you will reach out and minister to the broken hearts among you. I pray you will be filled with the compassion and creative energy you need to bring hurting survivors to the Lord for healing.

Church leaders and teachers, I pray that you will remember that in every group you lead, in every class you teach, there's almost certain to be someone who has experienced sexual abuse. Remember them. Keep them in mind when you're teaching, telling stories, and asking questions. You play a special role in their spiritual growth. Speaking insensitively can make them feel alone and unimportant, but speaking to their hearts with sensitivity and concern can make them feel safe and accepted, opening the door for healing to take place.

THE REST of the Story

The rest of Mark's story about the four friends of faith involves a double miracle—the healing of the paralytic and the forgiveness of sins:

> Seeing their faith, Jesus said to the paralyzed man, "My child, your sins are forgiven."
> But some of the teachers of religious law who were sitting there

DON'T JUST do church, go out and be the church.

thought to themselves, "What is he saying? This is blasphemy! Only God can forgive sins!"

Jesus knew immediately what they were thinking, so he asked them, "Why do you question this in your hearts? Is it easier to say to the paralyzed man 'Your sins are forgiven,' or 'Stand up, pick up your mat, and walk'? So I will prove to you that the Son of Man has the authority on earth to forgive sins." Then Jesus turned to the paralyzed man and said, "Stand up, pick up your mat, and go home!"

And the man jumped up, grabbed his mat, and walked out through the stunned onlookers. They were all amazed and praised God, exclaiming, "We've never seen anything like this before!"

—Mark 2:5–12

In this story, Christ proves that He has the power to forgive sin by showing that He had the power to heal the paralyzed man. When Christ heals, He aims at healing the entire person—body, soul, and spirit. Our problems and needs run deeper than we sometimes know, but when we come to the Great Physician, He diagnoses accurately and heals completely. When we see Christ doing this, we can't help but be amazed and praise God.

The way to true healing is through true faith. Jesus always responds to faith, whether it's the faith of the one who needs healing or, as in this case, the faith of his friends. People who don't think they need a physician don't want to come to Christ for healing. But those who have been humbled by suffering do want to come, and true friends of faith are willing to help them.

Margaret Mead, the famous anthropologist, once said, "Never doubt that a small group of thoughtful, committed citizens can change the world. Indeed, it's the only thing that ever has." If you feel that your church community isn't holding out a lighted torch, not being Christ to the abused and hurting, don't just complain about it. Don't just *do* church, go out and *be* the church. Someone once said that when good people do nothing, evil survives. So—for heaven's sake—do something! Like the paralyzed man's friends of faith, be creative and assertive and persistent. Be the first to make a difference. Bring the matches and then be the air that fans the flame into a fire.

Once you take that step of faith, don't let every little setback make you draw back in fear. God will keep your flame alive. If it's from Him, He will reward your obedience. As you continue to feed the flame with fresh air, it will take off, and you will see the light begin to flicker in the lives of broken people everywhere.

A Life Letter

Dear Friend of Faith . . .

One of the things I most adore about Jesus is His desire to be with the broken. While He was on earth, He didn't write off hurting people or avoid them. He didn't focus on why they were broken—whether it was due to their own sin or some sin against them—He just wanted to be with them so He could heal them. Once you recognize Jesus' amazing love for the people society considered "unclean," you'll understand why many of the religious folks of the day opposed Him.

This attitude is still around in churches today. Yet as followers of Christ, we should long to tell the broken what we know of God's desire to heal them. Jesus has given us this good news and commanded us to pass it on. We are to do this not only with words, but also in deeds that demonstrate His power and love. So how do we do this? How do we invite broken people into our lives? I think that, as individuals, it takes constantly reminding ourselves what our own lives would look like if it weren't for the transforming work of Jesus. It is this realization that gives us ears to hear their stories and a heart that wants to get to know them instead of making snap judgments about them.

After we've invited the broken into our own lives, we need to begin thinking about ways we can create spaces in our churches for them. Recently someone in our city who had never attended our church described it as "the place where sinners go." I love that! God's main instrument for healing is, in fact, His church. We don't make room for broken people because we condone sin, but because we have the power in Jesus that can set them free from whatever holds them in bondage. The church is meant to be the place where sinners go. It makes no sense that the Jesus of Scripture would have it any other way.

Maybe you're someone who has a heart for women who are struggling with sexual brokenness, even though you yourself have never struggled in this area. That is my story. Along with a couple of other women in my church, I started a recovery group for these women, all of whom thought they were the only ones who were struggling in this area. They weren't and they aren't. They may not have their lives together—and that can cause some to consider our church "messy"—but they know that they need a doctor and that in our church, the Doctor is in.

As you look around your church, ask yourself, "Where are the sick?" If you don't see them, they either aren't coming because there is no place for them, or they're hidden within your walls. There are people in your church with porn addictions, people dealing with same-sex attraction, people who have been abused or are currently being abused, people who are sinning sexually as a result of their wounding. The list could go on and on. Give these people a safe space to struggle. Invite them in and love them. Fight alongside of them and for them.

The good news of Jesus isn't "good luck until you get to heaven," but "the Kingdom of God is breaking into the now!" Jesus longs for His kingdom to break into every life to reverse the effects of sin and death. He longs for the broken to receive His healing. He longs to see them free from shame and make them free to love and trust people. He wants to begin today. Won't you join Him?

—Sara

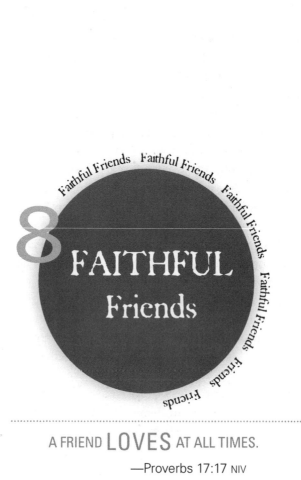

8

FAITHFUL
Friends

Faithful Friends Faithful Friends Faithful Friends Faithful Friends Friends Friends

A FRIEND LOVES AT ALL TIMES.
—Proverbs 17:17 NIV

I think that the English language can sometimes make it difficult for survivors to know how to show love in a way that will enable us to thrive in our different relationships.

In English we have only the word *love* to describe our deepest feelings of affection for others. For example, in conversations with my husband, I can say, "I love you," "I love my brother Garrett," "I love my friend Laura," or "I love survivors of sexual abuse." Since he knows me well, Matt would understand exactly what I meant.

However, in communicating with others, Greek would be better, for I could choose one of four different words to make it clear exactly what kind of love I'm talking about. I would use *eros* to indicate that I'm talking about the passionate, physical love I feel for Matt, *storge* to refer to the familial affection I feel for Garrett, and *phileo* to express the fond feelings I have for Laura. However, I would use *agape* to refer to the kind of love that I feel for survivors of sexual abuse. This kind of love involves my complete soul—my emotions, mind, and will.

When the New Testament talks about love, it almost always uses the words *phileo* and *agape*. Of these two kinds of love, *agape* is the highest. When Jesus said that the two greatest commandments are to love God and to love others, this is the word He used (Matthew 22:37–39). While *phileo* is based mainly on feelings, *agape* is based on a deliberate choice. *Eros, storge,* and *phileo* are kinds of love that can lead us into relationships. However, the closer each comes to *agape* love, the more we will thrive in those relationships.

For a survivor, love that chooses to walk with us no matter the cost can seem like a fantasy. Even if we do experience it, the relationship can feel scary. But we have to allow it, believe in it, and hold on to it, for one of the things survivors need most on the healing journey is the selfless love of faithful friends.

SOMEONE WHO NEEDED
a Faithful Friend

The Bible tells the story of an unusual friendship between a woman named Naomi and her daughter-in-law Ruth. The story is unusual because Naomi was an Israelite, while Ruth was a Moabite. The nation of Moab rejected the true God and was generally an enemy of Israel.

In the days when the judges ruled over Judah, Naomi lived with her husband and two sons in Bethlehem. When a severe famine fell upon the land, the entire family left their home and went to live in Moab. While they were there, Naomi's husband died, leaving Naomi and her sons, who married women of Moab. One of the women was named Orpah; the other was named Ruth.

About ten years later, Naomi's sons also died. With their deaths, Moab was a bitter place for Naomi. In those days, a woman could survive only as a daughter in her parents' home, a wife in her husband's household, or a mother in her son's home. It was hard for Naomi to breathe the air in the place where her husband and sons—and thus her hope—had expired. So when she heard that the famine was over in Judah, she made up her mind to go home.

Naomi had won the affection of her daughters-in-law, and they decided to go with her. But they hadn't gone far before Naomi urged them to turn back. She was a widow, and a poor one at that. What did her daughters-in-law have to gain by journeying to Bethlehem with her? While Naomi hoped to find food there, she was too old to bear more sons for her daughters-in-law to marry. Their only hope for security was to return to their parents' house. She also hinted that she was not worthy of their affection, that something about her was bad, unlovable, and deserved punishment. "The hand of the

Lord has gone forth against me," she told them (Ruth 1:13 NASB).

Naomi's daughters-in-law wept and refused to leave her, but she kept on urging them until at last Orpah went back to her own people. It seems she had a *phileo* kind of love for Naomi, but her love wasn't the committed kind that took risks. Ruth, however, seems to have had an *agape* kind of love for Naomi, and she chose to risk her own future for the sake of her mother-in-law. She knew that Naomi deserved to be loved unconditionally, and she was committed to walking beside her and supporting her on her journey.

"Don't ask me to leave you and turn back," Ruth said. "Wherever you go, I will go; wherever you live, I will live. Your people will be my people, and your God will be my God. Wherever you die, I will die, and there I will be buried. May the Lord punish me severely if I allow anything but death to separate us!" (vv. 16–17). When Naomi realized how steadfastly Ruth loved her and how determined she was to go with her, she ceased urging her, and they went on together to Bethlehem.

Ruth is an example of the kind of committed, faithful friend every survivor needs.

CAN YOU RELATE?

After I finally broke the silence to my mother, I told a counselor and a couple of mentors about my abuse. The next summer, I shared my secret at church camp. However, no one from my school had been there. By the time I was in my senior year of high school, as far as I knew, it was still a secret to those I interacted with every day. It wasn't until three years after I broke the silence that I finally found the courage to tell my best friend, Laura, that my stepfather had sexually abused me.

I remember it well. Laura had invited me to sleep over. It was really late. All the lights were turned off. We were lying in her big waterbed talking about the usual: school, sports, boys. I can't remember how I brought up the subject, but I do remember feeling a burning sensation in my chest, an irresistible urge to let my secret out. I knew I was ready to open up and tell it to a friend.

I was very nervous about telling Laura what I had been through. Like most sexual abuse survivors who tell a friend for the first time, I was afraid she would think I was gross or that I had done something to deserve it. I was even more afraid that she would look at me differently or feel sorry for me. Laura saw me as tough, fun, silly, and often loud-and-crazy Nicole. And that was part of the real me. But there was that other part, the secret hurting part deep inside, and I was afraid that if I revealed it, it would change her entire perception of me. I didn't want my image ruined. I didn't want people to pity me. I didn't want my best friend to think I was messed up or to feel as if she had to act differently toward me. I was afraid that letting out my secret would change everything.

When I told Laura, she reacted, but not in the way I had feared. She cried. She was upset that I had been hurt. She couldn't believe I had kept this secret in for so long. She thanked me for telling her and asked me how I was doing. I was honest. I told her that I was afraid that she would look at me differently now.

"Why would I look at you differently?" she asked. "Your step-dad was the one who did it."

And contrary to my fears, she never looked at me any differently. Even today, Laura still sees me as the fun sometimes loud-and-crazy Nicole she has always known. The only difference is that now she also knows that I'm not as tough as I had pretended to be. She knows that every now and then I need a big hug.

WHY WE HAVE TROUBLE
Keeping Friends

As survivors, we sometimes know that certain people have the potential to become faithful friends, yet we push them away. Sometimes we run from a relationship with them because, based on our past experiences, we're afraid that as soon as we've become attached, the friendship will end.

At other times, we're not able to recognize that someone has the potential to be a faithful friend. Abuse produces a haze that obscures our view of relationships. We not only can't breathe, but we also can't see clearly anymore. Our pain clouds our vision, and we see everyone in light of our fear of being hurt and our need to feel safe. When we're not able to talk through our past and process our emotions, we look at ourselves and others through a distorted lens. We see every relationship in light of the impact that sexual abuse has had on us. This is why healthy relationships are crucial. They provide us with a true mirror that reflects us back to ourselves.

If we don't run, we go to the opposite extreme and cling to try to ensure that the one person we've been able to relate to won't leave just as everyone else has. In the end, the result is the same. Feeling suffocated, the person leaves, and the relationship ends.

In an e-mail to me Cassie said, "I have a hard time opening up to anyone. So when I do, it's a big deal. But I have a problem in that, when I do open up, I get really attached to that person. I get ultra-sensitive about everything, almost like a little kid. I imagine this is annoying and probably pushes the other person away. And if the other person does something to lose my trust, I immediately push her away. It's frustrating, but I don't know how to change."

Tamara also had attachment issues. She noticed that in difficult times of healing when she had only one person in her life that she felt really close to, she quickly became obsessed with that person. She felt that she was nothing without the friendship and that her one friend was the answer to all of her problems. She made all her decisions based on her relationship with that one person and became jealous if her friend hung out with other people. This situation not only put a lot of pressure on that one friend, but also made Tamara overly dependent on her. This led to a one-sided, unhealthy relationship. A healthy friendship is a two-way street that involves both giving and receiving.

Ginger is a survivor who wants so much to have friends who will be sensitive to her needs and walk with her through the tough times, encouraging her and loving her. But she believes the lie that she is damaged and probably crazy and that no one would really want to be her friend. When I asked her if she has tried to develop any meaningful friendships, she said that she didn't even know where to begin.

My advice to Cassie, Tamara, and Ginger was the same: Begin by being a good friend to someone else. When you are a friend, you have a friend.

So many times I see survivors hiding in their box under the blanket, unwilling to even take a peek at what community has to offer. We will never know the friends that are available to us until we get out of our box and engage in community. So instead of focusing on your pain and sitting in hiding, afraid that no one will reach out to you (or if they do, that they soon will regret it), I invite you to reach out and be a friend to someone else.

It's hard to think about doing that, I know. It's scary to be so assertive and open about yourself. But I think that once you take that step, it will get easier and easier. You'll begin to see the impact it makes on others as well as on you, and you'll be proud of yourself for stepping out of hiding and engaging in a community.

BEING A FRIEND
to a Survivor

I remember being in college and wanting so much to talk to someone about all the stuff I was dealing with inside. I can still tell you the names of the few people who gave me an open door to talk with them if I needed someone to listen. And even though I wasn't quite ready to take them up on their kind offers, I always knew where I would go when I was ready to talk because I knew who wanted to listen.

Megan says that the main person who has helped her on her healing journey is her friend Andrea. "She was the first person I told at my school," Megan says. "She started out by listening to my story, and from that point on she listened whenever I needed someone to talk to. She always prayed for me, and when things got tough, she stood beside me. When I remembered being raped, she was there. When I shared my secret of cutting, she was there. She didn't look down on me or tell me to stop, even though I knew she wanted me to. She prayed for me and believed in me and supported me. To this day she listens and is there when I need a friend." As a faithful friend of a survivor, this is your role—putting the offer out there and being there when she is ready to open up to you.

I often speak to groups of student leaders, and the most common question they ask is: "What if I wonder if someone has been abused and I want to help them, but I'm not sure that they were?"

Maybe someone you care about is exhibiting some changes in behavior that raise red flags, or maybe he has made some comments that hint that he is hurting. First of all, thank you for being a person who is willing to be in close enough relationship with another that you would even notice a change in behavior. You've already invested something in this relationship, and now you're willing to go a step closer and reach out a helping hand.

In reaching out, never assume that someone has been abused without hearing it from his own lips. Never flat out ask him if he has been abused or push him to say anything about it one way or the other. However, I think it's appropriate to approach him privately and say something like this: "You've always seemed so outgoing, but lately I've noticed that you're quiet and reserved. Is everything okay? Would you like to talk?" Typically, he will respond with something like "Everything's fine." To which I strongly encourage you to say, "Okay, but I want you to know that I'm here for you and that I'm willing to be a listening ear if you ever need one." This says so much to someone who may have more pain bottled up inside than you could possibly imagine.

Remember: This is his story, so it's his choice about if and when he wants to share it with you. Everyone's journey is different. I simply encourage you to let this person know that you honestly care about him and then follow through by actually being there for him. Should he decide to talk later, he'll remember that you're willing to listen.

A survivor doesn't need to hear what you think she should be doing or how she should be reacting. A good counselor or spiritual mentor is the best person to help her in those ways. As her friend, you're there to journey with her, just as Ruth journeyed with Naomi. You're there to love and support her no matter what.

Shelly wanted to tell her best friend Jocelyn about the awful things that her older brother had done to her when she was a child, but she was afraid that her friend would abandon her if she knew. It was both a shock and great relief to Shelly when, after she told her friend this very personal story, Jocelyn not only believed her, but also thanked her for telling her, held her, and told her it wasn't her fault.

This is a great example of what a true friend does. Jocelyn didn't have all the answers—she may not have had any at all—but she loved Shelly and gave her what she had—her time and a listening ear. Besides listening, she also knew how to respond appropriately to what she heard.

If you're the friend who has had the honor of hearing a survivor break the silence about her abuse, hold your relationship with her very close to your heart. Survivors are often extremely selective about who will hear their story—so treasure the fact that she chose to tell it to you! Don't tell her that you can't handle it and that she needs to go to a counselor. She has chosen to confide in *you*. For some, just letting the secret out to a safe and trusted friend is everything they need for right now.

Crissy told me that her roommate is one of her most supportive friends. "Kendra really listens to me," she said. "She thinks about why I might feel or act the way I do, and then we talk about it. She doesn't try to 'fix' me or give me advice. Instead, she lets me talk through things to help us both understand why certain things resonate with me. One of the simple things she says to me is 'Crissy, that makes sense because of what you went through in your past.' That kind of confirmation means so much."

In my opinion, friend, you're capable of handling the situation simply by loving her, listening to her, and responding appropriately to what she tells you. That in itself is amazingly freeing. If it ever feels too much for you down the road, or if you know she's struggling with a death-dealing addiction, encourage her to talk to a professional counselor—and then go with her.

At the same time, if you're really uncomfortable about hearing your friend's secret, sensitively share that with her. Be sure you word it in a way that lets her know that you aren't uncomfortable with her, only with the issue. Explain why it's hard for you to hear, so she's sure it isn't her. Then offer to help connect her with someone who is comfortable with the issue and thus able to listen better than you can. Don't allow this to change your friendship at all. Be sure she sees that despite what you've learned about her pain, you're still the same friend you always were.

I'VE LEARNED that what survivors need more than anything else is not to just be heard, but to be heard and believed.

I've learned that what survivors need more than anything else is not to just be heard, but to be heard and believed. I think this is the best advice I can give a friend who has just heard someone's secret about being sexually abused as a child.

Survivors have an incredible fear of being perceived differently when a friend knows about the abuse. Heather wrote to me, "I love that you point out how important it is for people not to look at us differently after we share our secret. Why is that so important? I don't know—but it really is! I guess we take on the guilt of our abusers, and so it becomes shameful to us—as if there is something wrong with us because of what they did."

I agree with Heather. This is undeserved shame, and no one should look at us differently, whether in disgust or in pity. When this happens, it makes the abuse harder to deal with and more difficult for a survivor to want to tell anyone about it.

If you have a friend who confides in you about having been sexually abused, remember that this is something very personal and private. Disclosing it is usually accompanied by several strong emotions—relief, guilt, and fear now that someone else knows the secret. Please be a good friend and immediately reassure your friend that the abuse wasn't her fault, that she didn't deserve it, and that you don't look at her any differently because of it.

In some versions of the Bible, the word *agape* is translated as "charity," which comes from the Latin word *caritas*. Although the meaning of this word has changed over the years, it originally meant exactly the same thing as *agape*. As an acronym, CARITAS gives us an easy way to remember how to respond lovingly after a survivor breaks the silence:

Commend him for having the courage to tell.
Assure him that you don't look at him any differently.
Reassure him that he is safe now.
Insist that it wasn't his fault and that he didn't deserve it.
Thank him for trusting you enough to share his secret with you.
Affirm your commitment to care about him and to be a listening ear.
Show by your response how sorry you are that he went through this.

This is the way my friend Laura responded when I told her my secret. Since then, she has been a faithful friend through all my ups and downs. She now shares the joy I'm experiencing in an amazing ministry, a great marriage, and soon-to-be motherhood, but she also shared my pain along the way. She was there when I went through a rough period of unhealthy dating relationships. She told me the truth at times when I didn't want to hear it, but needed to. Though I got mad at her, she never stopped being real, never let me go, and never stopped telling me that I deserved better than what I was settling for at the time. She has deep respect for what I have come through in my life and how I use it to help others, and she has encouraged me when I've second-guessed God and doubted His plans for me. She has always believed in me. Laura has always been there to show me *agape* love.

We are called to great friendships—relationships in which our heart is knit together with others in a lifelong commitment to love. Our committed, *agape* love for others helps move them from desolation and despair to security and hope. Friends who show such love fulfill God's commandment to love Him and others, and He blesses their friendships.

THE REST of the Story

In her love for Naomi, Ruth made an irrevocable decision to journey with her wherever she went, loving and supporting her along the way. At first, Ruth's *agape* love didn't seem to make much of a difference in Naomi's life. Naomi was bitter and blamed God for the tragedy that had made her life harsh and empty. She was so focused on the relationships she had lost that she couldn't see the relationship she had.

When the two women got to Bethlehem, Ruth went into a harvested field to pick up the leftover grain. As it turned out, the field belonged to Boaz, a relative of Naomi's dead husband. A good man who knew what Ruth had done for Naomi, Boaz protected Ruth and provided for her. When Ruth told Naomi this, Naomi began to see things differently. "God hasn't quite walked out on us after all!" she said. "He still loves us, in bad times as well as good!" (Ruth 2:20 *The Message*).

Inspired by Ruth's example, Boaz became a part of Naomi's circle of inspiration. He married Ruth, and they had a son. God made up for the loss of the relationships from which Naomi had expected the most, and she ended up getting the most comfort from a relationship from which she had expected the least.

The story of Ruth shows us that we can make an astounding difference in a survivor's life by being a faithful friend. Ruth had vowed to never forsake the path she had deliberately chosen, and God rewarded her for her courage and constancy. Although she was a Moabitess, her love for and total devotion to her desolate mother-in-law made her a true Israelite and member of the family of God. In fact, she became the great-grandmother of David, the forefather of Jesus Christ. From a faithful friend, Ruth became a friend of faith.

A Life Letter

Dear Faithful Friend . . .

What I feel has helped the most in reaching out to my friend Jessica, is just being there and hanging out with her. If I notice that she's having a particularly hard day, I do something I know will make her smile. I send her an encouraging note and invite her to go for a walk in the park or to her favorite ice cream store. If she chooses to get together, I make sure to keep the conversation light and not try to be her counselor.

I've learned the hard way not to force Jessica to tell me things or do things she's not ready to do because that just seems to push her away. There have been times when all she needed was to be in my home, sitting on the couch watching TV. I've learned to let her be and not talk if she doesn't want to.

When she's ready, she'll speak, and I make sure she knows that when that time comes, I'll be there to listen. When she chooses to talk, I don't press for more details, even though sometimes I'm curious or the silence feels awkward. It was hard at first, but I've had to learn to be comfortable with silence. I'm also very careful not to make a big deal about what she tells me. As upset as it might make me to hear what she has been through, I try not to show it too much. I don't want to make her afraid to tell me things by panicking or acting shocked.

I try to be supportive, not overbearing. I keep connected to her, but I don't constantly check up on her or try to solve her problems for her. My job isn't to fight her battles for her, but to walk with her and work through her struggles together.

One of the significant things that helped Jessica move toward healing was for me to try to model Christ to her. Not that I'm perfect, but I tried to emulate Christ by being trustworthy, caring, loving, and comforting—the opposite of how she had viewed God in the past. Because many of her relationships had been unhealthy, the opportunity for her to experience a healthy friendship over time positively influenced her view of God.

Encouraging Jessica to talk to a counselor in addition to me was a big help. It was as if she, God, the counselor, and I were all working together toward a common goal. If you're committed to being a faithful friend to a survivor, don't be afraid to talk to a counselor yourself. Reaching out to a broken friend takes a lot of energy, time, and emotion, and you need support just as she does. Yes, it will be hard at times, but stick it out. Your friend needs you! Loyal friends are priceless treasures.

It's been awesome to watch Jessica move from silence to healing. She now has more confidence, can express her emotions, speaks truth to herself, and reaches out to others. She even carries herself differently. I've been able to see her come "alive" like a blossoming flower. In many ways it has seemed like a rebirth.

One thing to remember is that your friendship isn't all one-sided. As a faithful friend, you'll reap benefits along the way as well! Watching your friend progress in her healing, find freedom from her inner pain, and accept her true identity is something you can't put a price on.

—Courtney

9

SPECIAL
Friends

Special Friends Special Friends Special Friends Special Friends Friends Friends Special

THERE IS A FRIEND WHO STICKS
CLOSER THAN A BROTHER.

—Proverbs 18:24 NIV

As I write this, I've just reached the halfway point of my first pregnancy. Although it's exciting to be expecting, I must admit that it has had its challenges. Almost every morning for a couple of months, I found myself in the bathroom after breakfast, tossing my cookies into a porcelain bowl. As uncomfortable as that was, I'm sure that morning sickness is nothing compared to what I'll go through after my labor begins. When that time comes, I know I'll need my inner circle right there with me, praying for me, holding my hand, helping me breathe, and encouraging me to push through the pain to the blessed goal of bringing a new life into the world.

No one knows the value of a special friend more than a person who has chosen to step onto the road of healing. Healing from childhood sexual abuse creates a deep need for close relationships. Even when we have people around us who care, we need an inner circle of people with whom we can bond and bare our soul. Just as Jesus had His circle of three special friends, it's important for all of us to have the love and support of close friends. Without them, some of us wouldn't make it.

While God wants us to have these intimate relationships, He has given us boundaries for them because He loves us and knows what's best for us. When we cross His boundaries, problems start to arise, and if we aren't careful, our relationship can draw us off the road to life onto the road to destruction. If we are to thrive in our relationship with a special friend, we need to stay within God's boundaries.

When King David was old, he chose his son Solomon to succeed him as king of Israel. When he was about to die, he said to Solomon: "I am going where everyone on earth must someday go. Take courage and be a man. Observe the requirements of the Lord your God, and follow all his ways. Keep the decrees, commands, regulations, and laws written in the Law of Moses so that you will be successful in all you do and wherever you go" (1 Kings 2:2–3).

Solomon began his reign well. Because he loved the Lord, God appeared to him in a dream and said, "What do you want? Ask, and I will give it to you!" (1 Kings 3:5). Humbly admitting that he didn't know how to rule such a great nation, Solomon replied, "Give me an understanding heart so that I can govern your people well and know the difference between right and wrong" (v. 9). God was so pleased with Solomon's request that He promised him not only wisdom, but also fame, great riches, and a long life.

God kept His promises. Solomon became the wisest man who had ever lived, and he prospered in all that he did. As time passed, however, he began to make decisions that caused him to step outside of God's boundaries.

> Besides Pharaoh's daughter, he married women from Moab, Ammon, Edom, Sidon, and from among the Hittites. The Lord had clearly instructed the people of Israel, "You must not marry them, because they will turn your hearts to their gods." Yet Solomon insisted on loving them anyway. He had 700 wives of royal birth and 300 concubines. And in fact, they did turn his heart away from the Lord."
> —1 Kings 11:1–3

With *eros* clouding his reason, Solomon failed to heed all the Lord's commands, and his relationship with the women in his life drew him off the road to life onto the road to destruction.

"I wish I had someone who would support me on this path to healing while I'm at school," Kylie wrote me. "Phone conversations go only so far. Sometimes I just need to cry while someone lets me know that everything will be okay. Issues like the ones I'm dealing with seem to get pushed under the rug here. I've stopped going to most of my friends at school when I'm hurting because they just tell me I need to stop looking at all the negative things. I'm working on it, but there are still days—sometimes weeks—when the pain is all I can see. I hate pretending things are fine, but I can't risk losing the few friends I have here. I know the Lord brought me to this school, but it's hard with no really close friend."

Shortly after Kylie wrote me, she met Jeff, and they bonded immediately. Jeff was always there to listen when Kylie needed to talk, and he faithfully supported her on her healing journey. However, the relationship that was supposed to help her breathe soon began to suffocate her, stopping her short on her way to freedom.

"Our relationship created problems I never anticipated," Kylie later told me. "I started to look to Jeff for my identity, security, and self-worth, which eventually led to even more problems. As time went on, we became sexually involved. I thought that this would ensure that I'd never lose Jeff's love. Instead, it destroyed the very friendship I had been looking for."

WHY WE SOMETIMES TRESPASS
Boundaries in Close Friendships

Gender confusion caused by childhood sexual abuse is one reason survivors often step outside God's boundaries on the road to life. At a *Hush* book signing, I met a man who told me that because of the sexual abuse he suffered in childhood, he was so afraid that he was gay that he dove into the downward spiral of addiction to pornography. He said that he wanted to make sure he was attracted to women, not men, and this was how he decided to do that. His means of coping took over his life and made a mess of every relationship.

"My fear of being attracted to the same sex came from thoughts that kept running through my mind," Aaron said. "I didn't understand where they were coming from, and I sure didn't want them. I didn't realize that some of those thoughts were combinations of my past sexual abuse mixed with pornographic images and the lies Satan used to try to destroy my identity. My counselor has done a great job affirming me as a man made in the image of Jesus Christ. Jesus has begun to help me know who I am in Him, thus grounding all aspects of my identity."

Josh shared his story with me when I spoke at his university. He said that he figured he must be gay because the person who raped him was a man. If you have endured such abuse, you must always hold on to the truth: You didn't ask for it, you didn't want it, and just because you experienced it doesn't mean you are now somehow gay. We're all made in the image of God, and anything that says otherwise is a lie. Being a victim doesn't mean there's something wrong with you. There's nothing about you or in you that attracted the abuse. There's something wrong with the one who chose to abuse you.

I've met a number of victims of sexual abuse who, like Aaron and Josh, are confused about their sexuality. I find this happening most often when both victim and abuser were of the same sex. But this isn't always the case. A survivor who is struggling with and questioning her sexuality will inevitably carry this struggle into her close healing relationships, and without God as the foundation, those relationships will trespass His boundaries and self-destruct.

"I wasn't satisfied with my life or with God," my friend Maya says, "so I went searching for something to fill me. Due to a difficult relationship with my mother, I always looked to a female to fill me with the love that I felt I didn't receive in my childhood.

"When Sami walked into my life, she showed me so much love that I clung to it. I expected her to meet my every need and to satisfy my every desire. My life was consumed with her. I didn't want anything else, and I thought that she was all I needed to get through. All of my decisions were based on what she was doing. I had no life of my own.

"I never thought that using someone to meet my desires would leave me worse off than before—but it did. She was an idol in my life. She had full control over me, which in the end led to complete dissatisfaction and despair. Her love always left me feeling emptier than when I started. It always left me wanting more."

When we look to anyone to be our everything and the answer to all our problems, we are putting them in the place of God. And that is idolatry. We need close friends, but our intimacy with them should never replace our intimacy with the Lord. No matter how much we long for and need their love and support, we should never look to them for our total happiness and security. To put it simply, our needs should never make us needy, and we should never put our close friends above God. However, many of us seem to find this out the hard way.

"Sami and I had to stop seeing each other," Maya says. "There was no way that we could establish a normal healthy relationship after we both had crossed so many boundaries and convinced ourselves that this was the norm. Separating was the hardest thing that I have ever had to do, but I knew I had to do it. I had to learn to rely on the Lord for everything. Sami would never satisfy me no matter how much I wanted her to. That was God's place and His alone."

Losing yourself in someone else creates tunnel vision. And I'm not talking about the healing tunnel with the light at the end. I'm talking about a tunnel that points only to the person you're obsessed with. This tunnel isn't found anywhere near the tunnel of healing. In fact, it's found on the path of destruction, and the longer you choose to walk in it, the emptier and more miserable you'll feel, just like Maya. The more steps she took toward Sami, the further off the path of life she got. And she felt it. All the people in her other relationships felt it too.

I've found that most people who desire healing from the pain of their past also desire to be truly loved. Sadly for some of them, their strong desires can lead them to disobey the boundaries God has set for their own good. Childhood sexual abuse can make them unable to distinguish between *eros* and *agape* love, and like Kylie and Maya, they can get sexually involved with a close friend because they mistakenly think that sexual intimacy will give them the love they're looking for.

When we become close with someone who is willing to spend time with us and support us no matter what, it's easy for *eros* love to cloud our judgment, even though we may be doing our best to love with a pure heart. With all our good intentions, we can become more preoccupied with our own needs than with those of the other person, and this can make it impossible for us to show our special friend true *agape* love.

Freedom to thrive in a relationship is impossible when we are bound by what we expect a close friend to do for us. It requires a love that isn't concerned with filling our own needs. We must trust God to do that. The only special friend who deserves our unlimited devotion is Christ. People will always fail and disappoint us. They cannot satisfy. Their love will never, ever compare to God's love. It will only leave us wanting more. God has created us to need a greater more permanent love—His love. He is a friend who sticks closer than a brother, and we can have no greater friend than Him.

A special friend is a gift from God. We can ask Him for that gift, and He may choose to send us one in human form. If He does, it's our responsibility to keep our relationship pure. Satan will try to come into what could be a close, healthy friendship and tell us that we need more and that we'll never be satisfied until we have it. But the truth is that choosing what the Enemy wants us to long for will only lead to pain and destruction. We must choose not to walk on Satan's road, and that means we must know how to set appropriate boundaries.

HELPING SURVIVORS SET
Appropriate Boundaries

Survivors struggle with boundaries because at an early age someone who was responsible for teaching us healthy boundaries crossed the line himself. Now as adults, we live out what our abuser taught us. Some of us have no idea what healthy boundaries are. We need to be taught!

For many survivors, boundaries look like restrictions, and restrictions feel like rejection. But once we learn that boundaries are meant to protect what is good and that we are still loved and cherished, we're more willing to accept them and incorporate them into our own life. Far from strangling a close friendship, healthy boundaries breathe into it the love that enables us to thrive in it.

If you are a close friend of a survivor, there are two important ways that you can help her learn to set healthy boundaries. First, you can share with her what the Bible has to say about close, healthy friendships.

Jonathan's relationship with David is a perfect picture of what our own special friendships need to look like today. It's a picture of a godly friendship characterized by sacrificial love. God gave David a special friend in Jonathan because He knew that David was going to have trouble breathing. He saw the turmoil ahead of David and graciously provided him a loving friend to see him through it all. God brought Jonathan and David together to enhance each other's lives, and they repeatedly laid down their own desires for the other. Their love was true *agape* love.

A truly close relationship is characterized as much—or more—by giving as by receiving. Knowing the magnitude of God's love for us frees us from placing demands on our friend. It frees us from our insatiable need to be cared for and sets us free to care about others. It frees us from an inordinate need to be loved in return.

We know that we are showing *agape* love when we see our friend not as one who wants to meet our needs, but as one whose needs we want to meet so she can become everything God intends her to be. A special friend is someone who takes her hand during the dark, painful times in life and encourages her to keep breathing and pushing toward the goal when she wants to give up. A special friend sees the goal, the light at the end of the tunnel, and daily reminds a survivor of the promises God has given her.

The proof of Jonathan's love for David was that he never stopped giving of himself so that David might become what God intended him to be. Without Jonathan, David probably wouldn't have even survived long enough to fulfill God's plan for him.

Jonathan put his own life in danger so that David could keep breathing and pushing to the goal God had for him—to be the first in a line of kings that God intended to rule over His people forever.

A second way you can help a survivor learn to set appropriate boundaries is to teach her by example. Survivors of abuse can gain so much from healthy male and female role models. They learn a great deal just by observing clear and appropriate boundaries in a relationship.

"I wish every survivor could be blessed with a couple of special friends like I had," Skye says. "They were two trusted peers who were a couple years ahead of me in school. They helped me process my emotions and gave me wise counsel about so many things, including how much of my story to reveal or not reveal, and they bolstered my courage to speak out. I knew I could give one of them a call or fire off an e-mail when I was struggling with memories and such. One was a survivor and understood what I was dealing with; the other, who was fortunate enough not to have been abused, helped me to know what was 'normal' for women to struggle with and which struggles were probably related to past abuse.

"My friends felt comfortable following their hearts and being honest with me about their own needs and boundaries. They felt free to be realistic about how much time they could give me and to say no when they couldn't genuinely give themselves to me in a particular way. By establishing healthy boundaries with me, they enabled me to set healthy boundaries with others."

Parents—real and surrogate—can make a huge difference in the life of a survivor by not only loving and caring for them but also by being an example of a healthy relationship. They can demonstrate to sons how to respect women and to daughters how to respect men.

Susan says that two people who were a tremendous help to her were a couple at the church she attended while she was in college. "They had a son a little older than me and a daughter quite a bit younger," she told me, "but they treated me as one of their own. So all through college I had a set of 'parents' right there in town who loved me and supported me. Through them I got to see what a healthy marriage can look like and especially what a good father is. I'm so grateful for them, especially now that I'm married!"

SURVIVORS OF abuse can gain so much from healthy male and female role models.

Seeing healthy boundaries helps survivors know where they begin and end in relationship to others. It means that they know who they are, that they are secure in their uniqueness, and that they aren't dependent on others for their identity. In a healthy special friendship, there's a clear line that indicates where one person ends and the other begins. But when this line is missing, a survivor often looks to her special friend to fill her, especially during times of loneliness on the path of healing. Like Maya, she wants to lose herself in that friend—and her friend to lose herself in her as well—as a way of filling her void. This is always detrimental to healing and destructive of the friendship.

It takes time and practice to learn what we should have been taught in our childhood. Just as learning a new language is easier as a child than it is as an adult, so is learning to establish boundaries in close relationships. Like many survivors of childhood sexual abuse, I grew up lacking the ability to set and communicate my own boundaries. I also grew up confusing my worth with my sexuality. The result was that as a teenager, I truly believed that if a guy didn't want to be sexually intimate with me, he didn't really like me.

Sometimes I allowed myself to get too physically intimate with guys I dated. However, I never actually crossed the line because I knew what God's Word said about sex outside of marriage. I wanted to be a "good Christian girl," and I was afraid of the consequences. And, to be honest, I was just plain afraid to have sex. So I always said no, and that kept me safe in my close relationships. However, I began to thrive in those relationships only when I chose to make God's boundaries my own out of love instead of out of fear.

"There is no fear in love," the apostle John wrote. "But perfect love drives out fear, because fear has to do with punishment. The one who fears is not made perfect in love" (1 John 4:18 NIV). Perfect love means "complete" or "mature" love—*agape* love—and we learn to love God and our fellow man with this kind of love only as we grow in our relationship with Christ. As we do, *agape* love drives out the dread of God's just punishment, which so often drives us from Him. We move from obeying God out of fear of the consequences of disobedience to obeying Him because we love Him and want to do only those things that strengthen our relationship with Him.

The purpose of God's commandments is to get us safely to the light at the end of the tunnel. When God gives instructions about boundaries, He often does so in a general way. He expects us to study His commands and then apply their spirit and intent to our changing circumstances as we walk the path of healing.

Honoring the spirit of God's law is a heartfelt response to God's love for us. That, in turn, gives us the confidence to love our special friends as Christ loves us and frees us from fearing that they will reject us if we don't live up to their expectations. Learning how to set healthy boundaries and then how to adjust them during seasons of growth and change leads to heightened self-esteem, greater intimacy, and the freedom to thrive in relationships with special friends.

THE REST of the Story

God had promised the entire kingdom of Israel to the descendants of David forever, if only they remained obedient. Shortly before he died, David had reminded Solomon of this promise. He remembered his own sin with Solomon's mother, Bathsheba, and he wanted Solomon to not give in to the sexual sin that had already brought so much heartache to his family.

But as wise and as blessed by God as Solomon was, he eventually allowed *eros* love to prevail over *agape* love. He broke God's specific commandment to any man He called to be king of Israel: "The king must not take many wives for himself, because they will turn his heart away from the Lord" (Deuteronomy 17:17). For all his wisdom, Solomon was ultimately ensnared by the power of physical love, and as he added wives, he ended up loving them more than he loved the Lord. Ultimately, he found himself burning incense at the altars of pagan gods.

As a result, God told Solomon: "Since you have not kept my covenant and have disobeyed my decrees, I will surely tear the kingdom away from you" (1 Kings 11:11). When Solomon allowed *eros* to rule in his relationships, he ruined the closest relationship he had—his relationship with God—and he failed to fulfill the plan God had for his life.

Agape love is the key to keeping our relationships pure so that we can fulfill God's plan for our life. This kind of love never trespasses God's boundaries or leads to behavior that He condemns. It never leads us into relationships characterized by sexual impurity or idolatry. It always leads us to walk the path of life on our healing journey.

As we learn to recognize the difference between healthy and unhealthy relationships and then choose to follow the right path, we will learn that we have no closer friend than God. He is the Friend that sticks closer than a brother, and as we obey the boundaries that He has set for our relationships, we will find freedom to thrive in them.

A Life Letter

Dear Special Friend . . .

If you are a special friend to someone who was abused as a child, I want you to know that I can relate. You see, I too have been called to be a special friend to someone who was horribly abused as a child. I also was abused as a child, and the Lord blessed me with some special friends when I was going through my own healing. So I understand your strong desire to do whatever you can to help your hurting friend.

The main thing I want to say to you can be summed up in a single sentence: Your friendship is very important, but no matter how much you love your special friend, it isn't your job to rescue her, relieve her pain, or repair her. These are things only the living God can do. They are much too big for you to take on as your responsibility. Will the Lord use you to help bring about these things in her life? He almost certainly will. The very fact that He has called you to be her special friend means that He will use you to be His hands and feet to her in real ways, whether it's by giving her a hug, holding her hand, listening to her, or always being there for her.

But here's the tricky part. You have to let God show you when and how to be His hands and feet. More important, you have to know when to get out of His way. I know this only too well because I made a lot of mistakes when I was learning how to be a special friend to someone who had been abused. I was so horrified by what she had been through that what I wanted more than anything was to remove her pain by being everything that she needed. But in trying to do that, I inadvertently assumed the role of God in her life, and that got us both off track.

There were many times when I was convinced that the Lord was moving much too slowly, and I was certain that I could speed up the healing process through my own efforts. I learned the hard way that as difficult as it was for me to see my friend in pain, I wasn't the one who could rescue her from that pain. Only God could do that. In stepping out of my place, all I had done was cause a mess and slow things down. Sometimes the best thing I could do for her was to get out of His way and let Him work in her life.

How hard it still is for me to admit that!

But here's the good news: We have a God of grace and for-giveness! In spite of my mistakes, He continued to bring healing to my friend and to use me as His hands and feet in the healing process.

Here are some practical things to keep in mind, special friend. First, keep things in order in your own heart and life. God is first, followed by your spouse and children, or whatever other God-ordained relationships you have. Then comes your friend. If think-ing about, taking care of, or being with your friend is taking prece-dence over these other relationships, things are out of order and you need to make some changes. Stay in your own place, and trust God with the details of your friend's life and healing. He is the great healer and restorer. Believe that and let Him work.

What a joy it will be to be a front-row witness as God heals your friend—as He most certainly will!

—Debbie

10

A
LOVING
Spouse

A Loving Spouse A Loving Spouse A Loving Spouse A Loving Spouse Spouse

HUSBANDS, LOVE YOUR WIVES, JUST AS
CHRIST LOVED THE CHURCH.

—Ephesians 5:25 NIV

Song of Songs is a beautiful depiction of biblical marriage. In it the bride speaks of her husband as her lover and her friend. This is so true of a healthy marriage relationship. To be honest, one of the biggest fears I had going into marriage was that being married was all about having sex. Thankfully, that is simply not true. It's about being both friends and lovers.

We've seen how essential it is for survivors of sexual abuse to have friends in their circle of inspiration who are committed to traveling the road to healing with them. Of course, a spouse needs to be this kind of friend—a friend whose *agape* love never fails. But marriage is also based upon *eros* love. "It is not good for the man to be alone," God said (Genesis 2:18), and so He made a helper for man, a female companion, intimate friend, and sexual partner.

The problem for survivors and their spouses is that childhood sexual abuse can greatly distort our view of ourselves as sexual beings. Whether our abuse was short-term or long-term, seductive or violent, it has affected how we view ourselves and how we view sex. Mix this distorted view with traumatic memories, and it's easy to see why our behavior can perplex our spouse. He may find it difficult to understand us, and lack of understanding can take a huge toll on the marriage unless a spouse knows how to balance *eros* love with *agape* love.

SOMEONE WHO NEEDED
a Loving Spouse

Luke tells the story of a virgin named Mary who was engaged to be married to a man named Joseph. In those days, engagement was a binding contract that could be dissolved only by divorce. It was like being legally married today, with one exception: during the first stage of the engagement, the couple lived apart and didn't have sexual relations. That was reserved for the second stage, when the man took his wife to live in his home.

Mary and Joseph were in the first stage of their engagement when God sent the angel Gabriel to give Mary some startling news.

> Gabriel appeared to her and said, "Greetings, favored woman! The Lord is with you!"
>
> Confused and disturbed, Mary tried to think what the angel could mean. "Don't be afraid, Mary," the angel told her, "for you have found favor with God! You will conceive and give birth to a son, and you will name him Jesus. He will be very great and will be called the Son of the Most High. The Lord God will give him the throne of his ancestor David. And he will reign over Israel forever; his Kingdom will never end!"
>
> Mary asked the angel, "But how can this happen? I am a virgin."
>
> The angel replied, "The Holy Spirit will come upon you, and the power of the Most High will overshadow you. So the baby to be born will be holy, and he will be called the Son of God." . . .
>
> Mary responded, "I am the Lord's servant. May everything you have said about me come true."
>
> —Luke 1:28–38

We don't know if Mary told Joseph about the angel's visit and the step of faith she had taken in agreeing to the divine conception. All we know is that when Joseph learned that Mary was pregnant, he was just as troubled as Mary had been when the angel appeared to her. Although Luke doesn't say how Joseph reacted to Mary's pregnancy, Matthew clearly indicates that he was planning to divorce her.

Joseph simply didn't understand what was going on. We don't know if he communicated any of his misgivings to Mary, but I can't help but wonder: Did Mary hold her breath as she waited to see what Joseph would do?

CAN YOU RELATE?

When she was a child, Su's father sexually abused her. When she was a teen, he raped her. Her family didn't believe her or reach out to her; instead, they left her to fend for herself. Su said that after she got married, "Whenever my husband said anything that reminded me of my father, I would yell and freak out on him. And when we made love, I often saw my father's face. We loved each other and didn't want to divorce, but we had to separate because it was too much for our marriage."

For his part, Su's husband wondered what had happened to the woman he had married. He didn't understand what she was going through. All he knew was that he felt as if he was married to someone else and he wanted his wife back. He wanted to know what he could do to fix things. He wished she could get over it and move on. He wondered if her pain would ever end. He felt neglected and as if his needs didn't matter anymore. He hadn't done this to her, and he didn't understand why he also had to suffer. He hoped the separation would help them work things out, but deep inside he questioned if their marriage would survive.

WHY MARITAL INTIMACY
Can Be Difficult

Sexual abuse drums into your mind the belief that sex is bad. And if sex is bad and you have sexual feelings, then it makes sense to think that you must be bad too. Hear me when I say this: You are not bad! You were created as a sexual being, and these feelings are part of your beauty as God's creation. Sex, the way God meant it to be, is not bad at all. In fact it's quite the opposite! It's a gift meant for enjoyment and oneness.

There is also a close connection between sex and pain. That's why survivors like Su so often develop problems in intimacy in marriage. Alexis says that sex feels like a violation and a betrayal of her body. She wishes more than anything that she would never have to be sexual again. Georgia has sex with her husband just to "get it over with."

For the sake of healing and a healthy sex life with their spouses, Su, Alexis, and Georgia needed to realize that what happened when they were violated wasn't really "sex" at all. It was abuse. It was rape. They didn't choose it, and they were powerless to stop it. Therefore, it had nothing to do with their sexuality or with sexual intimacy. What happened to all of us survivors deprived us of the ability to view our sexuality in a healthy way. Now we need to reclaim that ability. We need to get it back. In order to find freedom in this area, we have to retrain our mind to see sex as God meant it to be.

I know it takes time to view sex the way it was meant to be, especially if you've experienced sexuality in the way I did as a child. But don't let your abuser steal this important piece of your marriage any longer. Healing is available! By giving this area of your life the time and attention it deserves, you can have a healthy and fulfilling sex life with your spouse.

I encourage you to seek out a good counselor who can help guide you on this journey through sexual healing. In counseling you can come to understand how abuse affected you in this area, gain a stronger self-awareness and more positive view of your sexuality, and learn communication skills that can help make sex the enjoyable experience it was designed to be. Couple therapy can be very effective also, but it's important to realize that the survivor is the primary victim, even though at times the spouse may feel as if he is. Receiving counseling together was what helped bring Su and her husband back together.

If we are to heal, we must not only look at sex differently; we must also look at our spouse in a different way. The wounds we carry from the past often cause us to project our hurts and fears onto him, even to the point that we consider him an abuser as well.

We must remind ourselves that our spouse is not the guilty party. We must separate the past from present and place the blame where it belongs—on our abuser.

The Bible offers us a compelling image that we can keep before us as we begin to look at our spouse with new eyes. It's the picture of God's Son as our Bridegroom. It might sound strange to think of yourself as Jesus' bride, but that's just what Scripture calls those who believe in Him. Seeing Jesus as our Bridegroom not only gives our spouse a model to emulate, but also opens our eyes so that we can see Christ in him.

When Matt and I were planning our wedding, I told him that ever since I was a little girl, I had dreamed of being swept up in my new husband's arms and carried into the reception hall where the wedding supper was to be held. Taking his bride-to-be's not-so-subtle hint, Matt made my childhood dream come true at our wedding reception. He swept me off my feet, sprinted down the length of the reception hall, and carried me in his big strong arms to our places at the banquet table. All of our guests laughed and clapped. For me, this is both a wonderful memory of my own wedding and a preview of the day when Jesus returns as our Bridegroom to take us in His arms and carry us to our reserved places at the Great Wedding Feast.

God is love, and Jesus longs to create a love story with us. His love for us is so deep that He came to earth to sacrifice Himself so that we could be with Him forever. As our Bridegroom, He wants to be with us as we climb every hill and push through every valley on our healing path. At those times when we need to reach out to Him and let Him carry us, He is always there, ready to pick us up and carry us in His strong arms over the rough places. Jesus our Bridegroom is kind, gentle, and patient; He doesn't try to force love. He doesn't push His presence upon us or force us to be with Him. He waits for us to invite Him to receive His love. This is what Jesus our Bridegroom is like, and when we catch glimpses of Him in our spouse, we can be assured that he is trying his very best to be like Jesus, no matter how hard it may be for him to understand what's going on in our life.

UNDERSTANDING A SPOUSE
Who Is a Survivor

Have you ever been talking with a friend whose breath smells so bad that it makes you hold your own breath to keep from inhaling hers? Have you ever wanted to tell her that she has a problem, but aren't sure how and don't want to hurt her feelings? It's a tricky situation for sure. Many of us would probably prefer not to say anything, but in reality, the truly loving thing to do would be to quietly and sensitively bring the problem to our friend's attention. The same is true for talking with a spouse who is a survivor of childhood sexual abuse.

Sexual relations are what distinguish marriage from any other kind of intimate relationship and our spouse from any other member of our inner circle. God has made us sexual creatures and has given us sex as a wedding gift. It's not only the way we procreate, but also the ultimate expression of love for the one person God has given us as our life partner here on earth. Yet survivors of sexual abuse often have problems with sexual intimacy, and it may be just as hard for a spouse to talk about this as it would be for him to talk about his wife's bad breath.

It can come as a complete shock to learn that your spouse is a survivor of childhood sexual abuse. Your first reaction will probably be to wonder why she didn't tell you about it a long time ago. But what you need to understand is how personal, private, and petrifying this secret is to a survivor. There is never a good time to say something like, "Hey, I've been meaning to tell you that I was raped when I was nine" or "It's about time I told you that my father molested me for about seven years of my childhood." That's just something it's never easy to say.

Your spouse wasn't trying to deceive you by not telling you this highly classified secret. Perhaps she is only beginning to deal with it herself and is filled with pain and shame and afraid of rejection. Understand that whatever you may be feeling as a result of this disclosure, she is feeling much worse because she's the one who went through it.

Try not to focus on the shock of not having known about this until now. Instead, concentrate on the fact that the secret is now out in the open and that there's an opportunity for healing. Things will get harder for both of you before they get easier, but acknowledging the abuse will make your relationship much stronger in the end.

As the spouse of a survivor, you need to remember that what she needs most as you walk the healing path together is your loving understanding. Above all, this means never ceasing to be her faithful friend. Think about how Joseph treated Mary, even before he understood what was going on in her life.

As Joseph understood the situation, Mary was pregnant with another man's child, and according to Jewish law and custom, the right thing for him to do was to divorce her. The usual way was by public trial, which would have brought Mary great shame and humiliation. Despite the embarrassment and pain Mary's condition caused him, Joseph's love and compassion for her wouldn't allow him to treat her that way. He was still Mary's friend, and he dealt with her lovingly. Not wanting to disgrace her publicly, he decided to divorce her quietly. Like Joseph, you can choose to be a gentle and loving friend, even though you may not understand what is really going on and may feel like reacting in anger or frustration.

Assure your spouse of your love for her and that she is safe telling you about her pain. She will fear that you will be disgusted with her. Express concern and sympathy for what she has gone through. Hug her if she is responsive to that. Most survivors want more than anything to be held by someone safe as they share their secret. But don't force touch upon her. Some survivors can't handle touch while they are opening up about their abuse. Your job is to simply offer her your open ear and your open arms and allow her to decide how much she is willing to receive of either of them.

Many spouses of survivors tell me that the problems in their marriage all began to make sense once the secret was disclosed and healing began. A spouse's jealousy, feelings of inadequacy, attention seeking, and possessiveness are often reactions to a survivor's conditioned response to abuse. By helping your spouse get to the root of her behavior, you'll allow your marriage relationship to find healing as well. Once the roots are healthy, the rest of the tree will begin to revive. Your marriage will reap the reward and begin flowering in ways you never expected.

Years into their marriage, Mitch's wife, Molly, began working on her painful past. As she worked through her traumatic memories, she became emotional and unpredictable. To Mitch she seemed like a totally different person, and he couldn't handle the change. He wanted to make her feel better, but he didn't know what to do. So instead of comforting her and supporting her through these valleys of her healing, he separated himself emotionally from her. He told his wife that she needed to "deal with it." He didn't want to hear about it because it was in the past and he thought she should leave it there.

As Mitch ceased to be a loving friend, their marriage began to fall apart. Like most survivors who are dealing with unhealed memories, Molly found sexual contact difficult. This had nothing to do with Mitch and everything to do with the feelings and memories she was currently working through. But Mitch made things even worse by taking it personally. Believing that she was bad to begin with, now Molly also felt unwanted, and she completely closed down sexually.

Being an understanding spouse sometimes means putting sexual relations on hold for a season. Although this can be difficult on the human level, it can also heighten your receptivity to the voice of God. It was in such a situation that Joseph was able to discern the voice of God speaking to his difficult circumstances.

As Joseph was thinking about divorcing Mary, an angel of the Lord appeared to him in a dream. "'Joseph, son of David,' the angel said, 'do not be afraid to take Mary as your wife. For the child within her was conceived by the Holy Spirit. And she will have a son, and you are to name him Jesus, for he will save his people from their sins" (Matthew 1:20–21).

As soon as the angel revealed to Joseph what was going on in Mary's life, he dropped his plans to divorce her and took her home, thus completing the engagement period. However, he also opted to remain celibate until God's plan was complete and the child was born. This was an act of great faith and sacrifice on Joseph's part.

When your spouse is going through something you don't understand, treat her as Jesus would. Gently reassure her and allow her to take things at her own pace. There will be things you will be required to sacrifice for her, and this will sometimes include your personal needs and desires. Sacrifice is hard, but it's at the heart of what it means to love and serve others. With your patience and understanding, she can return to normal and healthy sexual functioning.

WHEN YOUR spouse is going through something you don't understand, treat her as Jesus would.

Peter said that a husband should treat his wife with understanding. "She is your equal partner in God's gift of new life," he said. "Treat her as you should so your prayers will not be hindered" (1 Peter 3:7). God calls us to be right in our relationships with others. Otherwise we will be broken in relationship with Him, and our prayers will be hindered. I believe the Lord reveals His care and concern for the marital relationship here and the importance of husbands treating their wives with sensitivity, consideration, compassion, and understanding.

When Mitch did not treat Molly that way, he found that his prayers were hindered and that his relationship with God suffered. He not only felt alone in his marriage; he also felt distanced from the Lord. It wasn't too long before he felt convicted, and he knew that in order to get right with God, he needed to get right with his wife. He either had to humble himself and submit to being her friend, or continue to require her to submit to his will, which was only making matters worse.

Looking back, Mitch says, "I didn't know the details surrounding Molly's sexual abuse before we got married. I still don't know all the details, but what I do know is enough for me to realize that the events were horrible and terrifying.

"I tend to see things in black and white, as if there's a simple, quick solution for every problem. So when I found out that Molly was abused as a child, I initially didn't understand why it should be a problem after so many years. I had to learn that her situation was beyond my ability to fix and that her healing had its own timetable.

"I realized that my lack of understanding didn't make the problem go away for anyone. I found myself asking, 'What if I had the same personality she had and what had happened to her happened to me. Would my attitude be so black and white?' The answer was no. I'd want my spouse to understand that to me it was a big deal, and I'd want her to comfort me through the healing process instead of placing demands on me."

Mitch approached Molly in love and repented of his unloving response to her need. Their relationship has since been rebuilt. She has made huge strides on her healing journey, and Mitch is grateful for the Lord's faithfulness as He waited for him to grow up and be the friend and lover he was meant to be to his spouse.

THE REST of the Story

A Jewish man could be very cruel to the woman he was engaged to if she was found to be pregnant with another's child. He could divorce her—or even have her stoned—and she would die in disgrace. But when Joseph awakened from his dream, he knew that Mary was expecting the child as a result of a divine miracle. The "power of The Most High" had overshadowed her, and she was going to bear the Son of God. So he took Mary home with him, preserving their marriage and the life of her unborn child.

If Joseph had taken a short view of their situation, all he would have been able to see would have been the gossip and condemnation of her neighbors. But through the eyes of faith, he took the long view. Joseph and Mary both believed that what the angel had said to them would be accomplished. Their complete faith in God and love for each other was what made their marriage work.

If you have a spouse who was abused in childhood, you probably feel inadequate, unqualified, and even unable to handle the challenges it can create for your marriage. But you can do it. Hold your wife's hand, look into her eyes, and tell her you love her. Tell her that she's worth it. Then take a deep breath and step out with her into the healing tunnel.

A Life Letter

Dear Spouse . . .

When you marry someone you love, you want to be everything that person needs. You want to fill all her voids. As a male, I think it's an innate part of our nature to be protectors and want to fully provide everything that our wife might need. But in the realm of sexual sin and more specifically, sexual abuse, our instincts to provide for every need and fix every broken part of our spouse's world can be not only damaging to us, but also an impossible task, fraught with pitfalls that will only lead to further hurt and disappointment for both the victim and the nurturer.

In looking back on my relationship with Nicole, it's clear that I never needed to play the role of healer in her life. In talking with her and hearing the thousands of stories that she hears each year, it's clear to me that many survivors rush into marriage because they think that's how they will achieve a sense of wholeness. These broken individuals are looking to another person to put them back together. This is destined for failure unless the true focus of healing is transferred from a spouse to God the Father.

When I read Nicole's book *Hush*, and as I have listened to her own past struggles and the way she has viewed men, I really don't know how I would have responded to her or what I would have done to make her trust me. Fortunately, this wasn't something Nicole and I had to work through while we were dating or after we got married. Long before she pursued me, Nicole had already taken the steps to pursue her healing journey. And boy, did she ever! Postponing potential marriage relationships as she worked through her healing journey was healthy preparation so that she could enter our marriage as an emotionally, spiritually, and sexually whole partner.

So, as spouses of victims of sexual abuse, if we aren't supposed to heal them or give them sexual wholeness, then what is our role? First, I think that if a victim is single, she should initiate her healing journey as Nicole urges in *Hush*. If she is already married, she needs to embark on the same journey, and her spouse needs to support her.

Those of us in supporting roles need to do just that. We need to be listening ears; we need to be comforters; we need to be gentle in the way we love; we need to let them know it wasn't their fault; we need to be patient; and sometimes we need to sacrifice our own needs. As a survivor gathers up the courage to tell her secret, we need to support that. When our spouse feels uncomfortable in a sexual situation, we need to listen and respect that. When new memories of a troubled childhood or relationship bubble to the surface, we need to be there to listen intently and love her through it.

In summary, our job is to listen and love. That's it. When I look at my relationship with Nicole, I feel that the best way I can help her on her journey is to do these two things. It's the survivor's job to take the steps toward healing, and it's God's job to heal. It's our job to listen and love. God made our part the easiest one.

—Matt

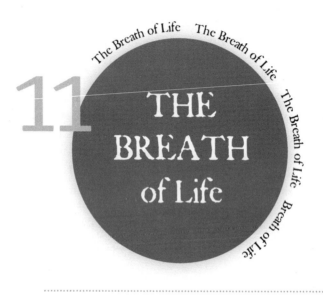

11

THE BREATH of Life

The Breath of Life   The Breath of Life   The Breath of Life   The Breath of Life   Breath of Life

THE **BREATH** OF THE ALMIGHTY GIVES ME **LIFE.**

—Job 33:4

By now it's clear that as survivors, we must surround ourselves with a circle of inspiration if we are to ever heal from our pain. But no matter how many people we choose to be part of it, it would still be incomplete without God. He is the only mandatory member of our circle. He is our Breath of Life, and if we truly desire healing, He must accompany us on our journey. Without Him, we cannot find the freedom to thrive in our relationships. Without Him, we cannot breathe.

Our entire existence began with a single breath—God's breath. Genesis 2:7 says that "the Lord God formed the man from the dust of the ground. He breathed the breath of life into the man's nostrils, and the man became a living person." We were nothing but dirt before God brought us to life through His breath. Because He has breathed His breath into each of us, we have a soul, which makes us unique among all living creatures. God has given us the ability to think, to feel, and to choose, powers of the soul that enable us to walk this journey of life in a very personal way.

However, simply being a unique human being God has breathed life into isn't enough for those of us who have to walk the challenging road of healing. For that, we need God to breathe on us again.

SOMEONE WHO NEEDED GOD
to Breathe on Him Again

After the crucifixion and resurrection of Christ, Peter desperately needed the Lord to breathe on him again. For three years, he had had an intense relationship with Jesus. Called to be a disciple, Peter was not only the leader of the Twelve, but also, along with James and John, part of Jesus' inner circle of three.

As one of Jesus' closest friends, Peter knew a lot about Him. When Christ asked the disciples: "Who do you say I am?" Peter could answer: "You are the Messiah, the Son of the living God" (Matthew 16:15–16). He knew that there was no one like Christ—that He was God in human flesh—and he even vowed to follow Him to the death. But when the time of testing came and Jesus was betrayed and arrested, Peter denied three times that he even knew Jesus. The third time, Peter exclaimed, "A curse on me if I'm lying—I don't know the man!" (Matthew 26:74).

It seems that Peter was telling the truth. He probably knew as much about Christ as any human being could, but he never really knew Him. And because he didn't really know Jesus, he didn't know the Father either. As a result, Peter's relationship with Christ wasn't what it ought to have been. Unable to follow Christ, he got off the road to life. To get him back on the right road, the resurrected Lord had to breathe on Peter again in order to show him who God really is.

CAN YOU RELATE?

Allie's abuser was her own father, who was supposed to be a man of God. As an Episcopalian priest, he was a father figure to her entire community. He was supposed to be a leading spiritual example, one who modeled the character of God. But his sinful actions completely distorted Allie's image of God, leaving her with a twisted and terrifying idea of who He really is. She grew up knowing all about Christ, but she didn't really know Him, so she never knew the Father either. All she could see was the example set for her by the man who should have shown her, as best he could, what God is really like. Allie wants to follow Christ. She wants to invite God into her circle of inspiration so He can hold her hand on her healing journey. But in her mind, God is like her father, and that makes it impossible for her to follow Him.

WHY IT CAN BE HARD
for Us to Follow God

Like Allie, we develop our first ideas about God through our parents, so if our earthly father is an abuser, our knowledge of God will suffer. If our beliefs about Him are based on our relationship with an abusive parent, we aren't likely to want to have a personal relationship with the only One who can genuinely heal us. To love and follow God, we must know who He really is.

If you were a victim of incest as Allie was, you may perceive God as scary and unpredictable. Julia believed that God was a perfect and inaccessible Someone sitting high above the clouds who wouldn't care about what she had been through or want to help her even if He did. Gwen viewed God as a judge who would always see her faults, view her as a failure, and want to punish her. Allie, Julia, and Gwen couldn't risk allowing God to be a part of their circle. In fact, they tried to keep Him out at all costs.

Many survivors of childhood sexual abuse have misconceived notions of who God is. Because of the pain and trauma my stepfather's sin caused, I once had these kinds of false beliefs and more. I made God what I thought He must be based on my experience of abuse. But in judging Him, I also shut Him out. I cut myself off from His breath. When I retreated to my little box and taped it shut, I didn't give Jesus permission to breathe on me, and without His breath, I was suffocating. I just didn't know it at the time.

For too long I tried to keep my defensive walls built high. I didn't want to be vulnerable or uncovered. But even when I was hidden away in my box, Jesus saw me—the real me. And He loved me right where I was, just as I was. Even when I was preparing to reinforce my box, He was standing right outside, calling me to drop the tape, step out, and come to Him.

To know God, we must strip off all the things we try to make God, all the undeserved accusations we place upon Him, and every lie the world wants us to believe about Him.

Have you ever noticed that when you know people only from distance it can be easy to make judgments about them? I remember that when I was playing college basketball, many of the girls on my team, including me, made some of the cruelest assessments about certain players on other teams. Years after I graduated, I ran into some of those girls and spent some time talking with them and getting to know them personally. Much to my chagrin, I discovered that they were nothing like what my teammates and I had assumed they were from a distance. When I eliminated the space between us, it changed my perception of them.

The same goes with our understanding of God. The further away we are from Him, the more likely we are to have a warped perception of Him. The distance between us leaves room for deception, fear, lies, and doubt to crop up. But when we get close to Him, there's no space in between us where mistaken beliefs can take root. We can know Him personally, talk to Him, and get to know Him for who He really is, not for who others might say He is. The distance we maintain from God is Satan's playground. To know Him we must eliminate the space.

The truth is that we will never grasp all of who God is. He is bigger than we can imagine, and so is His love for us. Words cannot contain Him. Still, to know who we really are, we must seek to know God. Once we begin to know Him as He truly is, we have a better sense of how He looks at us. This is important, for His thoughts toward us will inevitably impact our view of ourselves and all our relationships.

Scripture says that God is our Abba, our precious, loving Daddy. Some have said that the famous depiction of the Last Supper portrays the apostle John leaning over to Jesus to ask Him questions. Some versions of Scripture translate the Greek that way as well. However, *The Message* says that John was "reclining against" Jesus. I love that. To me, it depicts a loving dad whose chest I can lay my head against while I share my deepest secrets and ask Him about His dreams and plans for my life. Even more, it depicts a relationship in which I am free to invite Him to tell me about Himself.

When I recline against Jesus, I understand that God doesn't cause all the evil that occurs in this world. He doesn't cause all of the suffering in our lives. And He certainly doesn't cause sexual abuse.

In fact, He hates it! God is love, not pain. But pain can either bring us closer to Him or push us further away, depending on our response to it and whether we believe the truth about God or a lie. Painful circumstances can cause us to believe lies about God and walk away from Him. But when we step toward Him in faith despite our pain, miracles can happen.

Remember the woman who had been bleeding for twelve years? Her story is actually a story within a story, for Jesus healed her while He was on His way to heal someone else. Jairus, the leader of the synagogue, had come and knelt before Jesus. "'My daughter has just died,' he said, 'but you can bring her back to life again if you just come and lay your hand on her'" (Matthew 9:18). Jesus was on His way to the girl when the bleeding woman touched His robe. After healing and blessing her, He continued on to Jairus's house, where He found a crowd weeping and wailing.

"Why all this commotion and weeping?" Jesus asked. "The child isn't dead; she's only asleep" (Mark 5:39). The mourners laughed at Him, but after Jesus had sent them all outside, He took the girl by the hand and said, "My child, get up!" (Luke 8:54). Immediately, the little girl stood up and began walking around.

I believe that Jesus will do the same for us today. Once we step out in faith and place our burden at His feet, our Lord will breathe on us again and say to us, "My child, get up!" No matter how others have treated you, no matter how unworthy and undesirable you may feel today, no matter how you have thought of God in the past, you are His child, and He will help you get up from your bed of brokenness and pain and begin walking in a new relationship with Him. I believe Jesus wants to give sexual abuse survivors a second wind.

Over time, God helped me see how my misconceptions about Him were squeezing the life out of my relationships, my self-image, and my future. Above all, they were keeping me from following Jesus. That's why I find Peter's story such a comfort. He, too, needed to see how his misconceptions about Christ were preventing him from being everything God intended him to be. In Peter, I see myself; and in the way Christ related to him, I see the way God wants to relate to all of us. Just as I see Him breathing new life into Peter,

I see Him breathing on me and other survivors of sexual abuse.

When I removed the tape and found the courage to climb out of my box, something happened that I hadn't expected. The Lord met me and loved me and changed me in ways no one else ever can or will. Let me tell you, once you encounter the amazing love God has for you, you'll never be the same. And when you're changed, you'll want to follow Him no matter what.

Once I got to know God, I couldn't believe I had tried to get through life without Him for so long. I wanted more and more of Him. I wanted Him to be everything in my life. And by surrendering my own desires and plans, it was as if I was not only inviting Him to tell me the way I should go on my healing path, but also giving Him permission to take my hand and walk with me the rest of the way. Oh, how I wish I had done that earlier!

HOW GOD BREATHES
on Us Again

When Peter saw the empty tomb on Resurrection Sunday, he believed that Jesus had risen from the dead, a fact that was confirmed when Jesus appeared to him later that same day. Yes, Peter believed—but he still went and hid. On Sunday evening, there he was with nine other disciples and a few other believers who had locked themselves in the upper room because they were scared to death of the Jews. But why was Peter there? In the garden of Gethsemane, he hadn't hesitated to cut off the ear of the servant of one of the Jews who had come to arrest Jesus. Peter was brave. So why was he hiding? Could he possibly have been hiding from Jesus?

Although Jesus has shown us the kind of relationship God wants to have with us, when we are hurt and confused, we tend to run away from Him. Out of fear, we lock and bar the door to keep Him out. But Jesus wants us to love and trust His Father as He does. We must let Him in, for He is the Breath of Life. If we are to truly embark on our healing journey, we're going to have to invite Him in so that He can breathe on us again.

Though the door was locked and barred, Jesus suddenly

appeared in the room and said, "Peace be with you." Since the disciples had deserted Jesus when He was arrested, they most likely expected the Lord to rebuke them. But Jesus wasn't there to reproach them; He was there to reconcile them. Their faith wasn't burning brightly, and Jesus showed up to reignite it. "Peace be with you!" He said again. "As the Father has sent me, so I am sending you." Then He breathed on them and said, "Receive the Holy Spirit."

Just as God's breath had given them life, so the breath of His Son was going to give them new life. When Jesus breathed on the disciples, He was promising them the power they would need to do the work He was calling them to do. His breath was a down payment on the Holy Spirit He was going to send after He returned to the Father. Meanwhile, His followers were to wait for this power.

Sometime after the risen Lord appeared in the upper room, He manifested Himself again to seven of the disciples on the shore of the Sea of Galilee. They were there because Peter had decided to return to what he knew best—fishing—and the others had followed him.

Like Peter on that terrible night, some of us stray from the road of life that Christ has made possible and step onto side roads by focusing on other things and other people instead of on Him. Even when we've been on the right path for a while, there may still be times when we decide to walk the road alone and go our own way, and that sometimes lands us on the road to destruction.

When that happens, just remember that God is patiently and lovingly looking to you, ready to extend His hand of grace, forgive you, give you the peace that comes from reconciliation, and help you back onto the right path. I sometimes picture Jesus walking up and down these paths we've created for ourselves. I see Him pursuing us in the most desolate areas and in the darkest streets. He is pursuing us because He wants us to have the life we've always dreamed of. That's the same reason He pursued the disciples.

They had spent all night fishing, but without success. Jesus called to them, "Children, you do not have any fish, do you?" (John 21:5 NASB). Of course, He already knew the answer. (I mean—hello—He's *God!*) So He told them where to cast their nets. Rather than pointing out that they were supposed to be waiting for the power He had promised instead of going out on their own hook, the Lord spoke to them as sons and helped them catch some fish—153 fish, to be exact! That was enough to convince the disciples that the stranger on the shore was Jesus.

After breakfast, the Lord got down to the reason for His visit. Peter's denial had ruptured his relationship with Christ, and Jesus had come to get him back into a right relationship with Him so he could do what God had called him to do. There was one qualification for this work—complete devotion to God. So Jesus asked Peter three times, once for every time Peter had denied Him, if he had this qualification (vv. 15–17).

"Simon son of John, do you love me more than these?" He asked. The Lord was really asking not one, but several questions. He was asking Peter if he loved Him more than the other disciples loved Him. He was asking Peter if he loved Him more than he loved fishing or anything or anyone else. And by using the word for *agape* love, He was asking Peter if he loved Him with all his soul. Was Peter completely sold out? Did he love the Lord with everything in him? Were his mind, emotions, and will completely committed to Him?

Peter's answer showed how his failures had humbled him. He was honest. He didn't claim, as he once had, to love Jesus more than the other disciples did. He didn't claim to love Him with the highest kind of love. Using the word for *phileo* love, he simply said, "Yes, Lord, you know that I love you."

"Then feed my lambs," Jesus told him.

Jesus phrased His second question in a simpler way. "Simon son of John, do you love me?" Again He used the word for *agape* love, and again Peter responded with the word for *phileo* love. "Yes, Lord," he said, "you know that I love you."

"Then take care of my sheep," Jesus said.

Both times, Peter was telling the truth. As his denial of Christ had shown, he was not yet totally devoted to Christ. The third time the Lord asked Peter if he loved Him, He met Peter right where he was and used the word for *phileo* love.

Peter was hurt that Jesus asked the question a third time, for

Jesus seemed to be saying, "You deserted Me, remember? I don't think you even have *phileo* love for Me." When Peter replied, he basically asked the Lord to look at his heart instead of his behavior. Still using the word for *phileo* love, he said, "Lord, you know everything. You know that I love you."

Then Jesus said to him, "Feed my sheep."

> SURVIVORS of sexual abuse can find healing and wholeness by allowing the Lord to be the uniting Person in their circle of inspiration.

Technically, Peter didn't qualify for the job. Since Peter could claim only *phileo* love for Him, Jesus could have stopped right there and said, "Okay, then, you're out. You aren't fit for the great purpose I had planned for you. Too bad. Sorry. See ya."

But Jesus didn't say that. He knew Peter's heart, and He was going to use him just as he was. He knew that Peter would grow into *agape* love, and that he would do so through suffering. And so He said, "Follow me" (v. 22).

In their meetings after the Resurrection, Jesus breathed new life into Peter. He reconciled him, restored their relationship, and recommissioned him solely on the basis of love. God the Father relates to us in the same way. He comes looking for us, cares for us, and works to get us in a right relationship with Him so we can follow Him. He doesn't require us to be perfect. He accepts us wherever we are, just as we are. He doesn't reject us because of our failures. He doesn't cast us aside because of our brokenness. Instead, He gives us opportunities to affirm our love for Him and begin the work He has called us to do and to live the life He has called us to live.

God deals with us as Jesus dealt with Peter. How do we know that? Because one of the most important things Jesus did while here on earth was to show us who God really is. John 14:9 clearly states that if we've seen Jesus, we know exactly what God is like. God doesn't hide Himself from those who want to find Him and know Him. And the more we know who He really is, the more new and exciting places He takes us, not only on our faith journey, but on our healing journey as well.

Survivors of sexual abuse can find healing and wholeness by allowing the Lord to be the uniting Person in their circle of inspiration. Without Him, we're like Peter was before the Lord breathed new life in him, merely walking in place, getting nowhere fast, or even going backward. We are breathless and lifeless and forever searching for something to fill us.

But when God breathes new life into us, even the most traumatic situations can be redeemed and the most broken of lives can be restored. When we boldly hop into Jesus' loving arms and run the race ahead of us, with the rest of our circle right there cheering us on, the pain of the past recedes and the light at the end of the tunnel gets bigger and brighter each step of the way.

THE REST of the Story

On the day of Pentecost, the Holy Spirit came upon a small gathering of believers in a dramatic and powerful way:

> Suddenly, there was a sound from heaven like the roaring of a mighty windstorm, and it filled the house where they were sitting. Then what looked like flames or tongues of fire appeared and settled on each of them. And everyone present was filled with the Holy Spirit and began speaking in other languages.
>
> —Acts 2:2–4

At the sound from heaven, Jews from every nation came running. They were amazed to hear the believers speaking to them in their native tongues about the wonderful things God had done. The sincere people in this crowd wanted to know the meaning of what they heard, while mockers just assumed that the believers had been drinking.

Then the disciples stepped forward, and a divinely energized Peter began to speak. His message was clear as he boldly proclaimed the truth about Jesus Christ. When he was finished, three thousand people came to know Jesus and became members of the body of believers. After receiving the Holy Spirit at Pentecost, Peter was changed. He no longer had a problem following Jesus.

In the Bible the word *breath* means the same thing as *spirit*. Just as loving Christ is at the core of having a relationship with Him, possessing the Holy Spirit is what enables us to follow Him. This is our Breath of Life, our Teacher, our Advocate, and our Guide as we move forward on the road ahead. When we invite Him into our healing journey, He gives us the courage to face the darkness ahead and the strength to leave things behind and overcome the obstacles in our path. He constantly reveals God to us and breathes His peace and power on the path we are walking. He gives us the freedom to thrive in all our relationships.

Psalm 34:4–5 (NIV) says, "I sought the Lord, and he answered me; he delivered me from all my fears. Those who look to him are radiant; their faces are never covered with shame." As we walk through the darkness of the healing tunnel, as we get to know God for who He really is, as we face our fears and are delivered from them, the Light at the end of the tunnel will get closer and closer and shine upon us, making our faces look radiant to those around us. We can release the shame we have carried far too long, walk free in the healing and grace that God wants to lavish upon us, and step into the unique purpose He has for our lives.

God's Spirit, His breath, gives us new life. Galatians 2:20 says, "My old self has been crucified with Christ. It is no longer I who live, but Christ lives in me." Receiving our second wind from the Breath of Life not only equips us for our personal journey through the healing tunnel, but also prepares us to minister to others we will meet along the way. If God has filled you with His breath, you can be sure He is calling you to breathe life into others.

A Life Letter

Dear God,

I praise You and thank You for the healing that is taking place in my heart and in my relationships. Thank You for providing me with a circle of inspiration for this journey. I pray that You will bless each one of them. Still, I know that no matter how many people I have in my circle, it would never be complete without You.

Lord, I desire healing, and I believe that You are the God who heals. I know that I need You in order to receive healing and to be free to breathe. I can't make this healing journey on my own. Purify me from my sin and the sin that has been inflicted upon me. Be my refuge and strength, my comfort and my guide as I journey toward wholeness. Help me to see myself with new eyes, Your eyes, and to hold tight to Your promises. Hold my hand as I walk toward Your light, and carry me when I can't take another step. Transform this wounded and calloused heart into a heart of flesh and blood that beats surely and strongly, all for You.

Father, I want to truly know You. I pray that Your breath will touch every inch of my being. In my pain and my attempts to cope, I have believed lie after lie, but I ask that You would shatter every single one that I have ever believed about You so that Your light of truth will be the only thing left shining down on me. Help me to carry Your love, Your truth, Your light into each of my relationships and into the world—a world that You created with a single breath. Help me to open my eyes to others who are hurting and broken and use me to minister to them as You have ministered to me. Fill me with Your breath of life that I might breathe into the lives around me.

I love You, Lord.
In Jesus' name. Amen.

Free to Breathe

I used to feel silly admitting that I'm afraid of the dark. It makes it sound as if I haven't grown up yet. But now I wish that all of us would admit that we're afraid of the dark. Why? Because I now know that we should be afraid of the dark!

The world we live in is full of darkness. It's all around us. Childhood sexual abuse is just one of many proofs of the utter darkness in our world. We're living in a murky fog, and, unfortunately, we're growing accustomed to it. But the longer we allow the works of darkness to continue, the darker our world will become. And as the haze thickens, it will get harder and harder for all of us to breathe.

For a long time my fear of the dark completely immobilized me. I didn't even want to breathe because I was afraid that whatever scary creature was lurking in the darkness would hear me. But I found that the longer I held my breath, the more my fear grew. I needed to allow my fear to drive me to action. I needed to focus on the ray of light shining beneath my bedroom door, take a deep breath, rise up from my bed of fear, and walk toward it.

It took a lot of inner strength to take the first step. But once I did, I found the courage to face my fear with more confidence. Each time I stood up to the darkness, I weakened the power that fear had over me. It became easier and easier to find my way to the light and open the door. That simple act gave me the power to shine light into all of the dark places where I was once afraid. It also gave me the courage to tell my secret, step out on my healing journey, and invite others to support me along the way.

Many times while I sat in fear in my darkened room, I longed to hear someone call for me and bring me out of the darkness. I wanted people who were in the light to invite me to join them where they were. I wanted to know I wasn't alone. And I wanted a helping hand to walk me out of there.

Survivors of sexual abuse, you need the helping hands that a circle of inspiration can provide on the journey to healing. Walking the healing path is difficult, and doing it alone can be very frightening. The darkness in the tunnel can make you afraid to breathe and freeze you in your tracks. But as your circle breathes new life into you, you'll find the courage you need to keep moving forward.

You should never cut yourself off from your circle completely, for you'll always need those relationships. However, you shouldn't allow them to become a crutch. There will come a time when the Lord will call you to allow Him to be the very air that you breathe. Heed His voice. Coming off life support is a victory for you and for everyone in your circle. So rely on the power that He has given you, look at how far you have come, and celebrate your recovery! Throw a party for yourself and your circle! Thank those who have helped you breathe along the way. And stay alert for other breathless, lifeless people who need the air your strong survivor lungs can provide them on their own healing journey.

When I think of the people I've walked with on parts of their healing journeys, I often think of 2 Corinthians 3:2–3, which says: "Your lives are a letter written in our hearts. . . . Clearly, you are a letter from Christ showing the result of our ministry among you. This 'letter' is written not with pen and ink, but with the Spirit of the living God. It is carved not on tablets of stone, but on human hearts." Like the stories of suffering people that we find in Scripture, the life letters of survivors are for all of us. God is writing all of our stories.

When I have the opportunity to hear another survivor's story, I don't just listen to it; I invite God to write it on my heart. Why? Why would I want to allow thousands of stories of pain and suffering to be written in my heart? Because each story is, or has the potential to be, a testimony of how God in His love and grace meets us here on earth in a very personal way. Every story reminds me of the very reason He has me reaching out to broken people—so that I might share in His story, so that I might help bring them closer to knowing Him. When we allow life letters—stories written by the Spirit of the Living God—to be written on our heart, we will be moved to do something to dispel the darkness of sexual abuse.

You may feel that your own life letter has only just begun to be written and that you can't possibly help someone else yet. But you can! Your open ear, your kind word, your time, your prayer, your touch, your act of service could be exactly what someone else needs to get through today. It could even make a difference for eternity. Who better to reach out and help another survivor begin writing her own life letter? The Lord wants to use you every step of the way. When you make yourself available to the people who cross your path, God will do the rest. You are there to help a survivor pick up her pen and put it to the paper; the Lord will do the writing.

WHEN WE allow life letters—stories written by the Spirit of the Living God—to be written on our heart, we will be moved to do something to dispel the darkness of sexual abuse.

Take the time to look around you. Do you see someone sitting fearfully in the dark? Whose path is about to cross yours? What is his story? You may have a split second to reach out to that person; don't miss it. You can be the voice that calls a survivor out of hiding. You can be the hand that helps her find courage to walk toward the light.

Yes, reaching out to the broken and abused can be risky, and it will cost you something. But the reward will be well worth it. As a speaker and author, one of my greatest joys in life is seeing isolated, addicted, and silently hurting people step out of their box and into the healing tunnel. But you, my friend, can have the even greater honor of being used for the long haul. You can be right there to see her free to breathe and thriving in all her relationships.

Should you make the life-giving decision to take up this challenge and enter into someone else's circle, I pray you'll give God the opportunity to also minister to you and stretch you along the way. Don't let your faith grow stale. Never believe you have all that you need. Don't let your pride or comfort rob you of what could be, both in someone else's life and in your own. There's always more to give and receive, and playing a supportive role in the life of a sexual abuse survivor may be the very thing God wants to use to uncover some things in your own life. Open your heart to what He may want to do in there. Trust me, you won't regret it.

Are you afraid of the dark? I hope you are. Because only those who are afraid of the dark will be inspired to shine the light that dispels it. You and I are called to be a light in this dark world. We're called to make a difference. We need to ignite the flame within us and then unite with others to reach into the darkest places around us. Pretending away the darkness or giving in to it by saying "This is just how it is" will only allow evil to grow. We must find the courage to face the darkness head-on in our own lives, and then we must come together to boldly shine light into the dark world we live in. Once the fog is lifted, we'll all be free to breathe.

In the Sermon on the Mount, Jesus said, "You are the light of the world" (Matthew 5:14). He wasn't speaking to a crowd filled with the rich, the beautiful, the successful, or the most influential people of that time. No. He was talking to the poor, the sick, the abused, the outcasts. He loved these people, and He loved them just as they were.

Jesus wants us all to know that no matter where we've come from or how we see ourselves today, we are a light to the world. The shadows that were cast into your life make no difference now. Jesus sees the light deep within you, and He invites you to see it too. So come out from hiding, my friend. Allow the Lord and those in your circle to help you uncover your unique beauty and worth. You are truly breathtaking. Your life letter is inspiring. The Light inside of you is and always will be stronger than the darkness around you.

So take a deep breath.

Seriously. Do it right now!

Ahhh . . .

Now go let your light shine and make a difference in this world!

HUSH

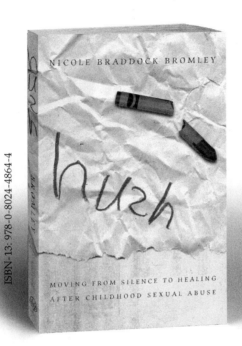

Childhood sexual abuse is running rampant, yet it's the best-kept secret in our nation today. Its victims grow into adulthood with their little child's heart trapped in the pain and torment of their past. Nicole Braddock Bromley shares her own story and the steps to moving from silence to healing. Hush exposes the harsh realities of childhood abuse, explains the pain it causes, examines the false beliefs it creates, and empowers survivors to begin a personal journey toward healing by breaking the silence.

MOODY
PUBLISHERS.

1-800-678-8812 · MOODYPUBLISHERS.COM

HIDDEN JOY IN A DARK CORNER

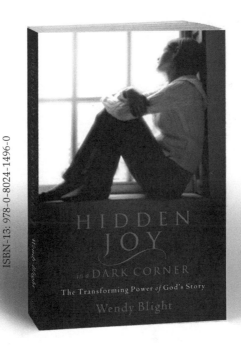

ISBN-13: 978-0-8024-1496-0

One week after Wendy Blight's college graduation, she walked into her apartment to find a masked man holding a knife and waiting for her at the top of the stairs. The man spent an hour physically and sexually assaulting Wendy, leaving her changed forever. After this terrifying experience, she lived for years cocooned in a prison of fear, despair, and hopelessness. Finally, after years of searching and believing she had nowhere else to turn, she fell on her knees before God and poured out her tears, anger, and questions to Him. Wendy's story is one of transformation from trauma to rebirth through the power of the Word of God.

1-800-678-8812 · MOODYPUBLISHERS.COM